D0482674

# A NEW OWNER'S
## GUIDE TO
# BASSET HOUNDS

JG-138

**Overleaf:** A Basset Hound adult and puppy photographed by Isabelle Francais.

**Opposite page:** A trio of Basset Hounds owned by John and Jackie Conway.

**The publisher wishes to acknowledge the following owners of the dogs in this book:** Patricia Alton, Mike Arruda, Diana Bartlett, Guillermo and Laura Borda, Lee and Debbie Coffer, John and Jackie Conway, Karen Curran, Patricia Czabator, Debbie Daniels, Carol B. Dappert, Renato DeGuzman, Terry and Marsha Emo, Ginnie San Fanandre-Russo, Scott and Deanna Fischer, Linda Fowler, Dorothy Lindsay Greynolds, Fred and Cindy Hastreiter, Janie Hemminger, Terri Hennessy, Lynn and Sarah Hollabaugh, Helene Hurford, Marsha Jacobs, Marit Jenssen, David and Barbara Keene, Dave and Geneva Kosh, Kelly McCoy-Davis, Christine McMahon, Harriet Micele, Allie Miller, Lynn Miller, Howard Nygood, Jennifer Parish, Rosemarie Peterson, Mike and Lori Pfeifer, William and Cynthia Pierce, Howard Schiede, Stephan and Alice Seiner, Grace Servais, Mary Smizer, William M. Stevens, Dawn Towne, Joan Urban, Clay and Cynthia Williams, Jane Wilner, Michaela Woiwode, Marina Zacharias.

**Photographers:** Paulette Braun, Bright Photo, Isabelle Francais, David Keene, Wayne Miller, Patty Sosa Photo, Robert Pearcy, Ginnie Russo, Vince Serbin, Karen Taylor, Jane Wilner.

The author acknowledges the contribution of Judy Iby for the following chapters: Sport of Purebred Dogs, Identification and FInding the Lost Dog, Traveling with Your Dog, Behavior and Canine Communication, and Health Care.

T.F.H. Publications, Inc.
One TFH Plaza
Third and Union Avenues
Neptune City, NJ 07753

ISBN 0-7938-2787-6

www.tfh.com

# A NEW OWNER'S GUIDE TO BASSET HOUNDS

## JOAN URBAN

# Contents

**2002 Edition**

**The Basset Hound blooms with character and friendliness.**

**Basset Hounds are skillful hunters and treasured companions.**

4

The Basset's long low body has helped him sniff out and locate game.

The versatile Basset is pretty much a "go anywhere" kind of dog.

Puppies require a lot of rest—as well as a lot of exercise.

# HISTORY of the Basset Hound

---

As the mists of the dawn of civilization began to clear, man's major pursuit was that of survival. Providing food for himself and his family and protecting the members of the tribe from danger were about as much as early man could handle. At that same time, however, a relationship already had begun to form between man and one of the beasts of the forest.

There is little doubt that early man saw his own survival efforts reflected in the habits of this beast that made ever-increasing overtures at coexistence. That beast was none other than *Canis lupis*—the wolf.

The wolf families had already developed a cooperative and efficient system of hunting the food it needed for survival. Man was not only able to emulate some of these techniques, as time passed he found he was also able to employ the help of the wolves themselves in capturing the animals which would constitute a good part of his diet. Wolves saw in man's discards, a source of easily secured food and the more cooperative wolves found they had increasingly less to fear of man. The association grew from there.

The road from wolf-in-the-wild to "man's best friend," *Canis familiaris,* is as long and fascinating as it is fraught with widely varying explanations. The wolves that could assist man in satisfying the unending human need for food were of course most highly prized. It also became increasingly obvious as the man-wolf relationship developed through the ages, that certain descendants of these increasingly domesticated wolves could also be used in survival pursuits other than hunting. Some of these wolves were large enough and strong enough to assist man as a beast of burden. Others were aggressive enough to protect man and the tribe he lived with from danger. In our study of the Basset Hound however, it is the wolf's inherent ability to scent and pursue that is of greatest significance.

In their enlightening study of the development of the dog breeds, *The Natural History of Dogs,* authors Richard and Alice Feinnes classify most dogs as having descended from one of four major

*The Basset Hound's unusual, soulful features make him one of the most distinctive breeds in the world today.*

groups: the Dingo Group, the Greyhound Group, the Northern Group and the Mastiff Group. Each of these groups trace back to separate and distinct branches of the wolf family.

The Dingo Group traces its origin to the Asian wolf (*Canis lupis pallipes*). Two well-known examples of the Dingo Group are the Basenji and, through the admixture of several European breeds, the Rhodesian Ridgeback.

The Greyhound Group descends from a coursing type relative of the Asian Wolf. The group includes all those dogs which hunt by sight and are capable of great speed. The Greyhound itself, the Afghan Hound, the Borzoi and Irish Wolfhound are all examples of this group and are known as the Coursing Breeds. They are not true Hounds in that they do not hunt by scent.

The Arctic or Nordic Group of dogs is a direct descendent of the rugged northern wolf (*Canis lupis*). Included in the many breeds of this group are: the Alaskan Malamute, Chow Chow, German Shepherd, and the much smaller Welsh Corgi and Spitz type dog.

The fourth classification is the Mastiff Group which owes its primary heritage to the Tibetan wolf (*Canis lupis chanco* or *laniger*). The great diversity of the dogs included in this group indicate they are not entirely of pure blood in that the specific breeds included have undoubtedly been influenced by descendants of the other three groups.

The descendants of the Mastiff Group are widely divergent but are known to include many of the scenting breeds—breeds which

*This Basset, owned by Marit Jenssen, looks right at home pictured against the mountains of Norway.*

*Separated at birth? The Basset Hound's long, low, seal-like body has contributed to his reputation as a valued hunting dog.*

find game by the use of their olfactory senses rather than by sight. These breeds include those which we now classify as Sporting breeds and the true Hounds.

As man became more sophisticated and his lifestyle more complex, he found he could produce from these descendants of the wolf, dogs which could suit his specific needs. Often these needs were based upon the manner in which man himself went after game and the terrain in which he was forced to do so. Instead of keeping dogs which simply rounded up game and herded them toward the hunter, man was able to develop some dogs large enough and strong enough to bring down the stag, the elk or the wild boar.

Fowl and small game had to be pursued in a much more sophisticated manner. And this sophistication led to hunting as a sport rather than solely as a means of survival. By this time man's constant march to civilization had taken him to the 15th and 16th century. Farmland abounded throughout Europe and what was once large forest land had been cleared and fenced. Man now was becoming accustomed to working within specified limits. The dogs he used had the hunting instincts of the great hounds of the past but these newer hounds could be controlled by voice and horn. Rather than using just one dog to find and trail the game man was after, he used several such dogs—each to back up the other and thus avoiding mistakes and loss of the trail.

While not always the quickest to learn their roles, these scent hounds were valued because they stubbornly refused to be diverted once on the trail. These hounds would persist in plugging on to recapture the coldest of trails. These are characteristics that typify the scent hound of today. Often accused of being slower on the uptake than, say, a terrier, once the scenthound has made up its mind what the task at hand is, it is extremely difficult to dissuade the dog from its objective. The latter creates a special kind of persistence that must be dealt with intelligently on the part of the dog's owner.

In France, when hunting was the sport of the nobleman, the long-legged hound was preferred. The Revolution in 1789 was to change this preference. The hunter was far more apt to be the common man who accompanied his dogs on foot. He needed a dog that was strong enough and short-legged enough to conquer dense underbrush and whose skin was loose enough to slip and slide over the terrain rather than impaling the dog on the brush. This hunter was not after the stag. He sought smaller game, game that would provide his family's evening meal.

The short-legged dog that could easily keep its nose to the ground was given high priority. It was also believed the long ears of these trailing hounds helped channel the scent to the hound's highly developed olfactory system.

Thus was born the need and the proliferation of numerous good-sized, short-legged hounds who combined all the assets of size, strength and tenacity of their forebears with the exception of their height. Among them were several varieties of Basset. Four important ones were two wiry coated dogs, the Basset Griffon Vendeen and Basset Fauve de Bretagne, and two smooth-coated Bassets, the Basset Bleu de Gascogne and the Basset Artesien Normand. All of them measured under 16 inches and all were classified under the heading "bas," which in French simply means "low-set" or "dwarfed." Therefore, one had to be most specific in reference to which *Basset* was being spoken of. It is said the Basset Artesien (also referred to as the Basset d'Artois) in tandem with the blood of other French scenthound crosses contributed most heavily to the Basset Hound as it is known today.

The Basset Artesien was first shown in Paris in 1863 at the first dog show held in that city. Lord Galway purchased several breeding pairs and imported them into England. However, major credit for the development of the breed in England is given to Sir John Everett Millais.

Millais imported the outstanding male "Model," from France. Model was not only the first Basset shown in England but became the cornerstone of Millais's highly successful breeding program in which he crossed Model's blood with that of the Beagle and later the Bloodhound.

The Basset Hound was "officially" recognized as such by the kennel clubs in both America and England at approximately the same time, 1885 and 1887 respectively. Actually the Basset Hound had existed in both countries for many years before as popular pack hunters.

The first British Standard of the breed was printed in Hugh Dalziel's *British Dogs, Volume I* , which was published in 1879. England organized its first Basset Hound breed club in 1884, and popularity of the breed skyrocketed among field enthusiasts throughout England.

*The Petit Basset Griffon Vendeen, shown here, is one of the original variety of hounds that shares ancestry with the Basset.*

*The long-legged Basset-type hound was first popular in France, where hunting was considered the sport of noblemen.*

Unfortunately World War I brought exhibiting and breeding to a standstill except for Mrs. Elms of Reynalton Kennels fame and Miss Keevil of Grims Kennel, who fortunately continued on with their Basset Hounds, albeit at near-borderline subsistence level.

In America, the Westminster Kennel Club show offered a class for Basset Hounds in early 1884. The competition was won by a dog named Nemours, who went on to become a champion two years later.

The first Basset Hounds to be registered with the American Kennel Club were Countess and Bouncer. Both were several years old before they were actually registered in 1885. Countess was bred in Germany and Bouncer in America.

*The Basset Hound's popularity in America soared during the 1950s and 60s as dedicated breeders strived to improve the breed and gain worldwide recognition.*

Although the Basset enjoyed the support of its hunting enthusiasts, the road to acceptance as a show dog was long and slow. However, between 1935 and 1940 it appeared the Basset Hound was beginning to be noticed, and the Basset Hound Club of America was founded in 1935 to assist in the promotion and best interests of the breed.

The club held its first field trial at Hastings, Michigan in 1937. The trial was won by Hillcrest Peggy, owned by Emil and Effie Seitz—two of the BHCA founding members. Peggy was to become the breed's first Field Champion.

World War II curtailed show activities for Basset Hounds, as it did for all breeds of dogs. By 1946, however, peace had come to the U.S. and dog activities resumed with a new and growing interest in the Basset Hound.

In May of 1949, Anthony of St. Hubert, bred and owned by Mark Washbond, made his ring debut, and by September of that year "Tony" had acquired his championship. This was the dog that the Basset Hound world had waited for.

Tony was striking and charismatic. He was seldom ever defeated in breed competition and went on to win many Hound Groups.

In 1952 it happened. Tony won the first all-breed Best In Show ever for the breed! This win was at the Egyptian Kennel Club show under Carey W. Lindsay. The interest of the all-breed fancy was aroused and popularity of the Basset Hound soared amongst dog show exhibitors.

The 1950s and '60s proved to be Bassetdom's golden years. The breed's rise in popularity and its success in Hound Group competition attracted more and more experienced dog men and women from other breeds. These individuals, recognizing the importance of using only the best stock obtainable in their breeding programs, spared no expense or effort in establishing new and better breeding avenues to follow.

As a result of this increased interest, the BHCA was able to hold its first independent specialty show in Chicago, Illinois in the year 1955, with an overall entry of forty.

The breed's rising popularity was not without its down side of course. There were many who jumped on the Basset "band wagon" and bred for an exaggeration of the Basset Hound characteristics they saw the general public attracted to. This was at the expense of the breed's suitability for the field and even of the breed's health.

The field enthusiasts were not to escape the results of the breed's popularity either. There was that element in the field who felt they wanted a speedier dog to hunt with and began breeding a taller, more refined and completely out of character Basset to accomplish this.

*A pack of Basset Hounds enjoying a day in the field.*

*Basset Hounds have proven themselves to be loving and gentle companions.*

In response to these fads, really dedicated breeders then and to this day have been adamant in maintaining the Basset Hound's true mental and physical characteristics and have encouraged all owners to continue to work their dogs in the field. There is no title more coveted in Bassetdom than that of the Dual Champion. The winner of this title is a dog whose physical characteristics have earned him his AKC conformation championship and whose ability in the field has merited the title Field Champion.

The first Basset Hound ever to accomplish this important dual championship was Pat and Jim Dohr's Dual Ch. Kazoo's Moses the Great. Moses was a conformation champion in both the United States and Canada and had completed all of his titles by 1964.

Basset Hounds have now reached a level of quality that earns them Hound Group and Best In Show awards not only in the United States but throughout the entire world of dogs. Top-quality Basset Hounds are always heavy contenders in their show-ring competition with all breeds. However, the goal of the Basset Hound Club of America and of all genuinely dedicated Basset breeders is to maintain the duality of the breed—*loving and gentle companion and reliable and steady field dog.*

# CHARACTERISTICS of the Basset Hound

I f you are still in the "deciding" stage of whether or not you should bring a Basset Hound puppy into your life, our advice is, do not (we repeat *do not*) visit a kennel or home in which there are Basset puppies. You will not leave without one! Those soulful eyes and floppy to-the-floor ears make the little guys absolutely irresistible! Of the many breeds we have known in our lifetimes, we find none more captivating than the baby Basset Hound.

It is for this very reason the person anticipating owning a Basset Hound should give serious thought to the decision. Basset Hound puppies are the subjects for millions of picture-postcards, greeting cards and calendars each year. There is nothing more seductive than that sad-looking little pup looking up with those soulful "won't you please adopt me?" eyes. Innocence personified! But in addition to being forlorn and cute, Basset Hound puppies are living, breathing and very mischievous little creatures, and they are entirely dependent upon their human owner for *everything* once they leave their mother and littermates.

Buying any dog, especially a puppy, before someone is absolutely sure they want to make that commitment can be a serious mistake.

*It is almost impossible to resist this adorable bunch, but be sure to carefully consider your decision to take one home.*

*How can you deny this face anything? Bassets have that "look" that makes them hard to resist.*

The prospective dog owner must clearly understand the amount of time and work involved in dog ownership. Failure to understand the extent of commitment dog ownership involves is one of the primary reasons so many unwanted canines end their lives in an animal shelter.

Before anyone contemplates the purchase of a dog there are some very important conditions that must be considered. One of the first important questions to be answered is whether or not the person who will ultimately be responsible for the dog's care and well being actually wants a dog.

All too often it is the mother of the household who must shoulder the responsibility of the family dog's day-to-day care. While the children in the family, perhaps even the father, may be wildly enthusiastic about having a dog, it must be remembered they are away most of the day at school or at work. It is often "mom" who will be taking on the additional responsibility of primary care giver for the family dog. Somehow even the "working mom" seems to have this responsibility added to her already staggering load of duties.

Pets are a wonderful method of teaching children responsibility, but it should be remembered the enthusiasm that inspires children to promise anything in order to have a new puppy may quickly wane. Who will take care of the puppy once the novelty wears off? *Does that person want a dog?*

Desire to own a dog aside, does the lifestyle of the family actually provide for responsible dog ownership? If the entire family is away from home from early morning to late at night, who will provide for all of a puppy's needs? Feeding, exercise, outdoor access and the like cannot be provided if no one is home.

Another important factor to consider is whether or not the breed of dog is suitable for the person or the family with which it will be living. Some breeds can handle the rough and tumble play of young children. Some cannot. On the other hand some dogs are so large and clumsy, especially as puppies, that they could easily and unintentionally injure an infant.

Then too, there is the matter of hair. A luxuriously coated dog is certainly beautiful to behold but all that hair takes a great deal of care. At first thought, it would seem therefore that a smooth-coated dog like the Basset would eliminate this problem. Not so, as we will see. While there is no long hair to contend with, there is a great deal the Basset Hound owner is called upon to do in the way of skin care and cleanliness.

*In terms of grooming, the Basset Hound is a low maintenance dog. The time you want to spend grooming your dog should be a consideration when choosing a breed.*

As great as claims are for any breed's intelligence and trainability, remember the new dog must be taught every household rule that he is to observe. Some dogs catch on more quickly than others and puppies are just as inclined to forget or disregard lessons as young children.

*Make sure the whole family is willing to take on the responsibility of a new puppy. Richelle Russo with her best friend Casey.*

## CASE FOR THE PUREBRED DOG

Although all puppies are cute, not all puppies grow up to be the picture of what we as humans find attractive. What is considered beauty by one person is not necessarily seen so by another. It is almost impossible to determine what a mixed breed puppy will look like as an adult. Nor will it be possible to determine if the mixed breed puppy's temperament is suitable for the person or family who wishes to own him. If the puppy grows up to be too big, too stubborn or too active for the owner, what then will happen to him?

Size and temperament can vary to a degree even within a purebred breed. Still, selective breeding over many generations has produced dogs giving the would-be-owner reasonable assurance of what the purebred puppy will look and act like as an adult. Points of attractiveness completely aside, this predictability is more important than one might think. A person in training for the Olympic 100 yard dash and wants a dog to come along on those morning workouts is not going to be particularly happy with a slower-paced and short-legged breed like a Basset Hound. Nor would the fastidious housekeeper, whose picture of the ideal dog is one that lies quietly at the feet of its master by the hour and never sheds, going to be particularly happy with the shaggy dog whose temperament is reminiscent of a hurricane.

Purebred puppies will grow up to look like their adult relatives, and by and large, they will behave pretty much like their the rest of their family. Any dog, mixed breed or not, has the potential to be a loving companion. However, a purebred dog offers reasonable insurance that it will not only suit the owner's lifestyle but the person's esthetic demands as well.

## WHO SHOULD OWN A BASSET HOUND?

What kind of a person should own a Basset Hound? As much as we love and cherish these dogs, this is *not* a breed for everyone. There are many special considerations that must be taken into account before the decision to own a Basset Hound is made. Perhaps it is best to begin with a list of people who *should not* own a Basset Hound.

The Basset Hound is not the breed for someone who would be put off by getting slobber on their clothing or furniture. Basset Hounds, particularly the males, have large pendulous lips and they will often shake their heads so the slobber will *fly!*

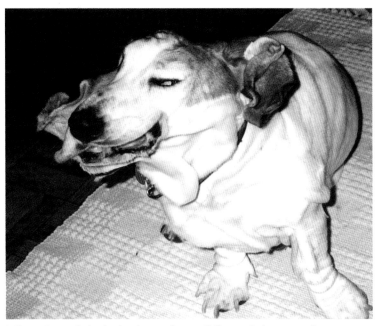

*When a Basset shakes his head, everything will fly—including a significant amount of slobber! Carly, owned by Dorothy Lindsay Greynolds, lets loose.*

The Basset Hound is not for an individual who is going to be offended by regularly having to clean a set of large, smelly ears.

Nor should anyone who doesn't want to keep their Basset Hound's ears up in a snood think about owning the breed. The only way to avoid having those ears drag through food, water or mud is to keep the ears up in a snood. Not doing so leads to trails of slime wherever your Basset will travel through the house.

If you are someone who wants a dog who lives to respond to your commands with hair-trigger speed, *forget about the Basset Hound*. Don't torture yourself with this breed. While it is true that some Bassets are easily taught and some do very well in obedience trials, as a whole the Basset is *not* the best choice for those who wish to become famous in obedience circles unless they are individuals who enjoy a real challenge.

A person who needs a small dog should not consider the Basset. This is a large breed. The only thing small about the breed is the distance from his elbow to his foot. A big dog on small legs best describes the breed.

The reason the Basset Hound looks so different from most other "regular" breeds is that he is a dwarf and, as such, many things about him *are* different from most other breeds. All too often people are attracted to the breed's beautiful, sad eyes and adorable, long ears and buy a puppy without thinking what it will be like to try and train a big dog on short legs.

Because Bassets are not easily trained, the traits that are bearable, even cute, in a puppy become absolutely unbearable in a 50- or 60-pound adult. The Basset's lack of enthusiasm in regards to training will often deter an owner from persisting in important household rules. Thus, the dog grows up without being lead broken or house broken. The untrained Basset can become a nuisance barker and a problem not only for the owner but for the owner's neighbors as well.

You would be amazed at how often it is necessary to rescue Basset Hounds from the animal shelters. More often than not these rescue dogs are there because the owner felt their dog was impossible to train when in fact it was the owner's negligence that led to the dog's bad manners.

On the other hand, the Basset is generally a very healthy dog. There is not a great deal of work involved in keeping the breed clean and healthy and Bassets have a temperament guaranteed to bring joy to your life!

Basset Hounds are natural comedians and are constantly getting themselves into hilarious situations that seem to delight them as much as they delight the people who own them. You will seldom be able to walk very far with your Basset without passersbys at least giving you a smile if not stopping you to chat a while.

Oddly, most owners hardly ever stop at just one Basset. Perhaps it's because Bassets are pack animals and seem to be more comfortable with another hound around. At any rate their owners seem to sense that and having raised one Basset, they immediately set about finding their next one.

### A BREEDER CHECK LIST

Just as the buyer should have a check list to guide him or her in locating a responsible breeder, most breeders have criteria that a buyer must meet before they would be considered an ideal candidate to have one of their puppies. These are things that a prospective Basset owner should be asking him or her self as well.

*Reputable breeders will be selective in choosing which adult Bassets to breed in order to produce the best puppies possible.*

**Yards must be completely fenced:** Bassets are often described as being loyal and although our egos would have us believe that our dogs would pine away if they were not with us, this is hardly the truth. A Basset could be just as happy anywhere as long as they were fed, loved, petted and had a couch or chair to sleep on. Bassets love people and therefore they are not adverse to accepting an invitation to take a stroll with a passing child or hop into the car of a total stranger. For this reason the Basset owner must have a securely fenced yard.

**No home where only one of the adults is enthused about getting a Basset Hound:** Owning a Basset Hound takes the cooperation of everyone in the household, and Bassets have very special and often very limited appeal. No Basset is safe in an environment that it is not *entirely* receptive.

**No home where children are solely responsible for the dog's care:** Bassets are very stoic and will take almost any abuse from a child. Parental supervision is an absolute must. While the best of children can love and care for their dogs they are not always capable of understanding or remembering the very special care Basset ownership entails.

**No home where they want to "get into breeding:"** Breeding Bassets takes a great deal of time, patience and hard work. It takes a long time to understand what kind of stock is even suitable for breeding and an even longer time to learn the intricacies of breeding, whelping and rearing a litter of Bassets.

# STANDARD for the Basset Hound

**G**eneral Appearance—The Basset Hound possesses in marked degree those characteristics which equip it admirably to follow a trail over and through difficult terrain. It is a short-legged dog, heavier in bone, size considered, than any other breed of dog, and while its movement is deliberate, it is in no sense clumsy. In temperament it is mild, never sharp or timid. It is capable of great endurance in the field and is extreme in its devotion.

**Head**—The head is large and well proportioned. Its length from occiput to muzzle is greater than the width at the brow. In over-all appearance the head is of medium width. *The skull* is well domed, showing a pronounced occipital protuberance. A broad flat skull is a fault. The length from nose to stop is approximately the length from stop to occiput. The sides are flat and free from cheek bumps. Viewed in profile the top lines of the muzzle and skull are straight and lie in parallel planes, with a moderately defined stop. The skin over the whole of the head is loose, falling in distinct wrinkles over the brow when the head is lowered. A dry head and tight skin are faults. *The muzzle* is deep, heavy, and free from snipiness. *The nose* is darkly pigmented, preferably black, with large wide-open nostrils. A deep liver-colored nose conforming to the coloring of the head is permissible but not desirable. *The teeth* are large, sound, and regular, meeting in either a scissors or an even bite. A bite either over-shot or undershot is a serious fault. *The lips* are darkly pigmented and are pendulous, falling squarely in front and, toward the back, in loose hanging flews. *The dewlap* is very pronounced. *The neck* is powerful, of good length, and well arched. *The eyes* are soft, sad, and slightly sunken, showing a prominent haw, and in color are brown, dark brown preferred. A somewhat lighter-colored eye conforming to the general coloring of the dog is acceptable but not desirable. Very light or protruding eyes are faults. *The ears* are extremely long, low set, and when drawn forward, fold well over the end of the nose. They are velvety in texture, hanging in loose folds with the ends curling slightly inward. They are set far back on the head at the base

*Author Joan Urban pictured winning with the very young homebred Fort Merill Fatal Attraction.*

of the skull and, in repose, appear to be set on the neck. A high set or flat ear is a serious fault.

**Forequarters**—*The chest* is deep and full with prominent sternum showing clearly in front of the legs. *The shoulders* and elbows are set close against the sides of the chest. The distance from the deepest point of the chest to the ground, while it must be adequate to allow free movement when working in the field, is not to be more than one-third the total height at the withers of an adult Basset. The shoulders are well laid back and powerful. Steepness in shoulder, fiddle fronts, and elbows that are out, are serious faults. *The forelegs* are short, powerful, heavy in bone, with wrinkled skin. Knuckling over of the front legs is a disqualification. *The paw* is massive, very heavy with tough heavy pads, well rounded and with both feet inclined equally a trifle outward, balancing the width of the shoulders. Feet down at the pastern are a serious fault. *The toes* are neither pinched together nor splayed, with the weight of the forepart of the body borne evenly on each. The dewclaws may be removed.

**Body**—The rib structure is long, smooth, and extends well back. The ribs are well sprung, allowing adequate room for heart and lungs. Flatsidedness and flanged ribs are faults. The topline is straight, level and free from any tendency to sag or roach, which are faults.

**Hindquarters**—The hindquarters are very full and well rounded, and are approximately equal to the shoulders in width. They must not appear slack or light in relation to the over-all depth of the body.

*The legs of the Basset Hound are short and sturdy and the hindquarters are full and well rounded.*

The dog stands firmly on its hind legs showing a well-let-down stifle with no tendency toward a crouching stance. Viewed from behind, the hind legs are parallel, with the hocks turning neither in nor out. Cowhocks or bowed legs are serious faults. The hind feet point straight ahead. Steep, poorly angulated hindquarters are a serious fault. The dewclaws, if any, may be removed.

**Tail**—The tail is not to be docked, and is set in continuation of the spine with but slight curvature, and carried gaily in hound fashion. The

*Basset ears are long and pendulous, hanging in loose folds with the ends curling slightly inward.*

hair on the underside of the tail is coarse.

**Size**—The height should not exceed 14 inches. Height over 15 inches at the highest point of the shoulder blade is a disqualification.

*Gait*—The Basset Hound moves in a smooth, powerful, and effortless manner. Being a scenting dog with short legs, it holds its nose low to the ground. Its gait is absolutely true with perfect coordination between the front and hind legs, and it moves in a straight line with hind feet following in line with the front feet, the hocks well bent with no stiffness of action. The front legs do not paddle, weave, or overlap, and the elbows must lie close to the body. Going away, the hind legs are parallel.

**Coat**—The coat is hard, smooth, and short, with sufficient density to be of use in all weather. The skin is loose and elastic. A distinctly long coat is a disqualification.

**Color**—Any recognized hound color is acceptable and the distribution of color and markings is of no importance.

**Disqualifications**—Height of more than 15 inches at the highest point of the shoulder blade. Knuckled over front legs. Distinctly long coat.

***Approved January 14, 1964***

# SELECTING the Right Basset Hound for You

The Basset Hound puppy you bring into your home will be your best friend and a member of your family for many years to come. The average well-bred and well-cared-for Basset can easily live to be eight, ten or even twelve years old. Early care and sound breeding is vital to the longevity of your Basset. Therefore it is of the utmost importance that the dog you select has had every opportunity to begin life in a healthy, stable environment and comes from stock that is both physically and temperamentally sound.

The only way you can be assured of this is to go directly to a breeder of Bassets who has consistently produced dogs of this kind over the years. A breeder earns this reputation through a well-planned breeding program that has been governed by rigid selectivity. Selective breeding programs are aimed at maintaining the breed's many fine qualities and keeping the breed free of as many exaggerations and genetic weaknesses as possible.

*Frida, owned by Marit Jenssen, nurses her four-week-old pups. Soon these puppies will be ready to go to loving homes.*

*To ensure against genetic disease and preserve the quality of their programs, reputable breeders will screen all Basset Hounds before breeding them.*

Anyone who has ever bred dogs will quickly tell you this selective process is both time-consuming and costly for a breeder and that no one ever makes money breeding sound and healthy dogs. One of the many things it does accomplish, however, is to ensure you of getting a Basset Hound that will be a joy to own. Responsible Basset breeders protect their tremendous investment of time and money by basing their breeding programs on the healthiest, most representative breeding stock available. These breeders provide each following generation with the very best care, sanitation and nutrition available.

Governing kennel clubs in the different countries of the world maintain lists of local breed clubs and breeders who can lead a prospective Basset buyer to responsible breeders of quality stock. If you are not sure of where to contact an established Basset breeder in your area, we strongly recommend contacting your local or national kennel club for recommendations.

There is little doubt that you will be able to find an established Basset breeder in your own area. Finding a local breeder will allow you to visit the breeder's home or kennel, inspect the facility, and in many cases you will also be able to see a puppy's parents and other relatives. Good breeders are always willing and able to discuss any

*Basset Hounds are always seeking affection—especially from their littermates. These two snuggle puppies are owned by Patricia Alton and Scott and Deanna Fischer.*

problems that might exist in the breed and how they should be dealt with.

If there aren't any Basset breeders in your immediate area, rest assured taking the time and exerting the effort to plan a trip to a reputable breeder will be well worth your while. If this is not possible, some breeders will arrange to ship a puppy to you by air. The shipping details are best discussed with the breeder you speak to.

Never hesitate to ask the breeder you visit or speak to on the phone any questions or concerns you might have relative to Basset ownership. Responsible breeders ask many questions of those who anticipate purchasing a Basset from them. Expect any Basset breeder to ask these and perhaps even more questions as well. Good breeders are just as interested in placing their Basset puppies in a loving and safe environment as you are in obtaining a happy, healthy puppy.

Not all good breeders maintain large kennels. In fact, you are just as apt to find quality Bassets come from the homes of small hobby breeders who keep only a few dogs and have litters only occasionally. The names of these people are just as likely to appear on the recommended lists from kennel clubs as the larger kennels that maintain many dogs. Hobby breeders are equally dedicated to breeding quality Bassets. A factor in favor of the hobby breeder is their distinct advantage of being able to raise their puppies in a home environment with all the accompanying personal attention and socialization.

Again, it is important that both the buyer and the seller ask questions. Be extremely suspicious of anyone who is willing to sell you a Basset puppy with no questions asked.

Do not just show up on the doorstep of a breeder's home or kennel. Call ahead and make an appointment at a convenient time so that you will be expected and not rushed.

### Recognizing a Healthy Puppy

Basset breeders seldom release their puppies until the puppies are at least eight weeks of age and have been given at least one of their puppy inoculations. By the time the litter is eight weeks of age, it is entirely weaned and the puppies are no longer nursing on their mother. While puppies are nursing they have a degree of immunity from their mother. Once they have stopped nursing, however, they become highly susceptible to many infectious diseases. A number of these diseases can be transmitted on the hands and clothing of humans. Therefore it is extremely important that your puppy is current on all the shots it must have for its age.

*Proper socialization with other dogs is very important for a well-adjusted puppy. These two Bassets are getting along just fine.*

A healthy Basset puppy is a happy, tail-wagging extrovert. Personalities and temperaments within a litter can range from very active to completely passive. Some puppies are ready to play with the world, others simply want to crawl up into your lap and be held. While you never select a puppy who appears shy or listless because you feel sorry for him, we would not hesitate to select the puppy who is calm and quiet just as long as he was healthy.

Taking a puppy who appears sickly and needy will undoubtedly lead to heartache and expensive veterinary costs. Do not attempt to make up for what the breeder did not do in providing proper care and nutrition. It seldom works.

If at all possible take the Basset puppy you are attracted to into a different room in the kennel or house in which he was raised. The smells will remain the same for the puppy so he should still feel secure, but it will give you an opportunity to see how the puppy acts away from his littermates as well as an opportunity to inspect the puppy more closely.

Above all, the puppy should be clean. The skin should be pliable and the coat smooth and soft. The inside of a healthy puppy's ears will be pink and clean. Dark discharge or a bad odor could indicate ear mites, a sure sign of lack of cleanliness and poor maintenance. A Basset puppy's breath should always smell sweet. The nose of the

*It's bedtime for these boys! Carol Dappert and Christine McMahon's red-headed twins do what Bassets love to do best.*

*The Basset Hound puppy you choose should be bright-eyed, healthy looking and happy.*

healthy puppy is cold and wet and there should be no discharge of any kind.

There should never be any malformation of the jaw, lips or nostrils. Make sure there is no rupture of the navel.

The puppy's teeth must be clean and bright and the eyes should be dark and clear. Runny eyes or eyes that appear red and irritated could be caused by a myriad of problems, none of which indicate a healthy puppy. Coughing or diarrhea are absolute danger signals.

While Basset puppies cannot be accused of being the epitome of style and grace, still their movement should be free and easy and they should never express any difficulty in moving about. Sound conformation can be determined even at eight or ten weeks of age.

The puppy's attitude tells you a great deal about his state of health. Puppies that are feeling "out of sorts" react very quickly and will usually find a warm littermate to snuggle up to and prefer to stay that way even when the rest of the "gang" wants to play or go exploring.

## MALE OR FEMALE?

The sex of a dog in many breeds is an important consideration and of course there are sex-related differences in the Basset that the prospective buyer should consider. In the end, however, the assets and liabilities of each sex do balance each other out and the final choice remains with the individual preference.

The male Basset simply has more of everything—more size, more weight—he's simply a larger dog to care for. He will mature somewhere between 50 and 70 pounds. More than just a handful for the average person. However, in the end, the male Basset makes just as loving and devoted a companion as the female. He can of course be a bit more headstrong as an adolescent and this will require a bit more patience on the part of his owner. Here again, the owner's dedication to persistence in training will determine the final outcome.

The male dogs of most breeds have a natural instinct to lift their leg to "mark" their territory. The male Basset is far less inclined to do so and those that have this tendency can usually be trained only to lift their legs outdoors.

Females have their semi-annual "heat" cycles once they have reached sexual maturity. These cycles usually occur for the first time at about nine or ten months of age. They last about 21 days and are accompanied by a bloody vaginal discharge for a part of that time. The discharge creates the need to confine the female to an area where she will not soil furniture or carpeting. There are also "pants" that can be obtained from your pet shop that will help avoid her "spotting" the area in which she lives. It must be understood the female has no control over this bloody discharge, so it has nothing to do with training.

Confinement of the female in heat is especially important to prevent unwanted attention from some neighborhood Lothario or she may become pregnant. Even a moment or two alone can result in an unwanted litter of mongrel puppies.

Both of the sexually related problems can be eliminated by spaying the female and neutering of the male. Unless a Basset is purchased expressly for breeding or showing from a breeder capable of making this judgement, your pet should be sexually altered.

Breeding and raising Basset Hounds should be left in the hands of people who have the facilities and knowledge to do the job properly. Only those who have the facilities to keep each and every puppy they breed until the correct home is found for it should ever contemplate raising a litter. This can often take many months after a litter is born. Most single dog owners are not equipped to do this.

Naturally, a responsible dog owner would never allow his or her pet to roam the streets and end his life in an animal shelter. Unfortunately, being forced to place a puppy due to space constraints before you are able to thoroughly check out the prospective buyer may, in fact, create this exact situation.

Parents will often ask to buy a female "just as a pet" but with full intentions of breeding so that their children can witness "the miracle of birth." There are countless books and videos now available which portray this wonderful event. Altering one's companion dogs eliminates bothersome household problems and precautions.

It should be understood however, that spaying and neutering are not reversible procedures. Spayed females or neutered males are not allowed to be shown in the conformation shows of most countries, nor will altered animals ever be able to be used for breeding.

## SELECTING A SHOW-PROSPECT PUPPY

If you or your family is considering a show career for your puppy, we strongly advise putting yourself in the hands of an established breeder who has earned a reputation for breeding winning showdogs. They and they alone are most capable of anticipating what one might expect a young puppy of their line to develop into when it reaches maturity.

Although the potential buyer should read the official standard of perfection for the Basset Hound, it is hard for the novice to really

*Breeding should be done only by people who have the facilities and knowledge to do the job properly. Pregnant mothers like Frida need extra special care.*

understand the nuances of what is being asked for. The experienced breeder is best equipped to do so and will be only too happy to assist you in your quest. Even at that, no one can make accurate predictions or guarantees on a very young puppy.

Any predictions a breeder is apt to make are based upon his or her experience with past litters that produced winning showdogs. It should be obvious the more successful a breeder has been in producing winning Bassets through the years, the broader his or her basis of comparison will be. "Quality begets quality" is an old stockman's adage that certainly applies in this instance.

The most any responsible breeder will say about an eight-week-old puppy is that it has "show potential." If you are serious about showing your Basset Hound, most breeders strongly suggest waiting until a puppy is at least four or five months old before making any decisions.

The standard has a very detailed description of how a top quality Basset should look and how it should move. Some things the complete novice can determine, other things take an expert's eye and even these are educated guesses when evaluating puppies.

The standard calls for a dark eye except that a lighter colored eye is acceptable but *not desirable* in a lighter colored dog. A novice would have little trouble in determining this point. However, evaluating movement is something that takes the experienced person's opinion.

There are many "beauty point" shortcomings a Basset Hound puppy might have that would in no way interfere with it being a wonderful companion. At the same time these faults could be serious drawbacks in the show ring. Many of these faults are such that a beginner in the breed might hardly notice. This is why employing the assistance of a good breeder is so important. Still, the prospective buyer should be at least generally aware of what the Basset Hound show puppy should look like and know what faults constitute "disqualifications" that would bar a Basset from being shown in conformation shows.

All of the foregoing regarding soundness and health in selecting a companion puppy apply to the show puppy as well. The show prospect must be sound, healthy and adhere to the standard of the breed very closely.

The complete AKC standard of the Basset Hound appears in this book; the more you know about the history and development of the

*Puppies require a lot of exercise, but they also need plenty of rest. This young Basset is just plain "flat-out" exhausted!*

breed, the better equipped you will be to see the differences that distinguish the show dog from the pet.

The things that really define a show prospect puppy are type, balance and temperament. Three simple words that have so many nuances it takes most breeders an entire lifetime to fully comprehend even a good part of them.

**Type:** Type includes the characteristics that differentiate the breed from all other purebred breeds. Paramount among these features of course are the Basset Hound's long head and ears. Short legs and a long body are two other things that also help establish the fact that this is a Basset Hound and not some other breed.

**Balance:** Balance is the manner in which all the desirable characteristics fit together. Their combination creates the picture of quality that says, "I am the best Basset Hound that ever was!" For instance, the Basset puppy's back is level without a dip or roach and it connects the puppy's two ends in such a manner that the youngster moves with ease.

**Temperament:** The correct Basset temperament combines all the wonderful characteristics that make him such a beloved companion. In the show ring the Basset Hound is a solid performer who moves about with a casual air and love of life.

*It is too early to evaluate these pups' show potential, but even if they do possess some faults, they'll still make wonderful pets.*

*If the show ring is in the future of the Basset puppy you select, it is best to wait until the puppy is four to six months old. This four-month-old pup is owned by Karen Currant.*

## PUPPY OR ADULT?

For the person anticipating a show career for their Basset Hound or for someone hoping to become a breeder, the purchase of a young adult provides greater certainty with respect to quality. Even those who simply want a companion could consider the adult dog.

In some instances breeders will have males or females they no longer wish to use for breeding or have developed some show ring flaw that diminishes their chances for a successful show career. On occasion a Basset is returned to the breeder because the owner moves or is no longer able to keep a dog.

Bassets of this kind could make wonderful companions for someone, and acquiring an adult dog eliminates the many problems raising a puppy involves. Bassets are a breed that can "transfer" well provided they are given the affection and attention they need.

Elderly people often prefer the adult dog, particularly one that is housebroken. The adult dog can be easier to manage requiring less supervision and damage control. Adult Bassets are less apt to be "chewers" and are usually more than ready to adapt to household rules.

There are things to consider, though. Adult dogs have usually developed behaviors that may or may not fit into your routine. If an adult Basset Hound has never been exposed to small children the dog may be totally perplexed, often frightened, by this new experience. Children are also inclined to be more active and vocal than the average adult, and this could intimidate the dog as well. Properly introduced and supervised, however, the relationship between dog and child will usually develop quickly and beautifully.

We strongly advise taking an adult Basset on a trial basis to see if the dog will adapt to the new owner's lifestyle and environment. Most often it works, but on rare occasions a prospective owner decides training his or her dog from puppyhood is worth the time and effort required.

## RESCUE DOGS

Sadly, many dogs are abandoned by their owners each year and end up in an animal shelter or dog pound. Other dogs wander away from home and strangely are never claimed by their owners.

B.H. Cares, Inc. is a nonprofit organization with chapters throughout the U.S. whose sole purpose is to find homes for rescued Basset Hounds. Rescued Bassets are from pounds or shelters or are strays whose owners cannot be found, or are relinquished directly by the owners who no longer want them.

*If you do not want to bother with housebreaking a puppy, an older Basset may be the right choice for you. Stanley is the beloved pet of Allie Miller.*

*Everyone loves Margaret! She became a BH Cares, Inc. rescue dog at nine years of age and has brought a world of devotion and companionship to her owner Patricia Czabator.*

If the original owners of the dogs B.H. Cares, Inc. deals with cannot be found, they are given a complete veterinary check-up and in most cases up-to-date inoculations are administered and the dogs are spayed or neutered. The dogs are closely observed to ensure their temperaments are suitable for adoption. The B.H. Cares, Inc. dogs are in need of good homes and could provide wonderful companionship for people who adopt them.

## IMPORTANT PAPERS

The purchase of any purebred dog entitles you to three very important documents: a health record that includes a list of inoculations, a copy of the dog's pedigree, and a registration certificate.

**Health and Inoculation Records:** You will find that most Basset breeders have initiated the necessary preliminary inoculation series for their puppies by the time they are eight weeks of age. These inoculations temporarily protect the puppies against hepatitis, leptospirosis, distemper and canine parvovirus. "Permanent" inoculations will follow at a prescribed time. Since breeders and veterinarians follow different approaches to inoculations it is important that the health record you obtain for your puppy accurately lists which shots have been given and when. In this way the veterinarian you choose will be able to continue on with the appropriate inoculation series as needed. In most cases rabies inoculations are not given until a puppy is three months of age or older

**Pedigree:** The pedigree is your dog's "family tree." The breeder must supply you with a copy of this document authenticating your puppy's ancestors back to at least the third generation. All purebred dogs have pedigrees. The pedigree in itself does not mean that your puppy is of show quality. All it means is that all of its ancestors were in fact registered Basset Hounds. They may all have been of pet quality.

Unscrupulous puppy dealers often try to imply that a pedigree indicates that all dogs having one are of championship caliber. This is not true. Again, it simply tells you all of the dog's ancestors are purebred.

**Registration Certificate:** A registration certificate is the canine world's "birth certificate." This certificate is issued by a country's governing kennel club. When the ownership of your Basset is transferred from the breeder's name to your name, the transaction is entered on this certificate and, once mailed to the appropriate kennel club, it is permanently recorded in their computerized files.

*The breeder will have started your Basset pup on the road to good nutrition, so stick to this original diet.*

Keep all of your dog's documents in a safe place as you will need them when you visit your veterinarian or should you ever wish to breed or show your Basset Hound. Keep the name, address and phone number of the breeder from whom you purchase your dog in a separate place as well. Should you ever lose any of these important documents, you will then be able to contact the breeder regarding obtaining duplicates

*Happy and healthy Basset puppies are a reflection of their breeder's good care.*

## DIET SHEET

Your Basset is the happy healthy puppy he is because the breeder has been carefully feeding and caring for it. Every breeder we know has their own particular way of doing this. Most breeders give the new owner a written record that details the amount and kind of food a puppy has been receiving. Do follow these recommendations to the letter at least for the first month or two after the puppy comes to live with you.

The diet sheet should indicate the kinds of food and number of times a day your puppy has been accustomed to being fed. The kinds of vitamin supplementation, if any, the puppy has been receiving is also important. Following the prescribed procedure will reduce the chance of upset stomach and loose stools.

Usually a breeder's diet sheet projects the increases and changes in food that will be necessary as your puppy grows from week to week. If the sheet does not include this information, ask the breeder for suggestions regarding increases and the eventual changeover to adult food.

In the unlikely event you are not supplied with a diet sheet by the breeder and are unable to get one, your veterinarian will be able to advise you in this respect. There are countless foods now being manufactured expressly to meet the nutritional needs of puppies and growing dogs. A trip down the pet aisle at your supermarket will prove just how many choices there are. Two important tips to remember: read labels carefully for content, and when dealing with established, reliable manufacturers you are more likely to get what you pay for.

## HEALTH GUARANTEE

Any reputable breeder is more than willing to supply a written agreement that the purchase of your Basset Hound is contingent upon his passing a veterinarian's examination. Ideally you will be able to arrange an appointment with your chosen veterinarian right after you have picked up your puppy from the breeder and before you take the puppy home. If this is not possible you should not delay this procedure any longer than 24 hours from the time you take your puppy home.

## TEMPERAMENT AND SOCIALIZATION

Temperament is both hereditary and learned. Inherited good temperament can be ruined by poor treatment and lack of proper socialization. A Basset Hound puppy who comes from shy or nervous stock is a poor risk as either a companion or showdog and should certainly never be bred. Therefore it is critical that you obtain a happy puppy from a breeder who is determined to produce good temperaments and has taken all the necessary steps early on to provide the early socialization necessary.

Taking your puppy to "puppy kindergarten" class is one of the best things you can do for him. There he will learn how to obey basic household rules as well as how to interact with other dogs and people. Your Basset puppy must learn to walk on a leash at your side without pulling and he needs to learn this *early*.

Temperaments in the same litter can range from confident and outgoing on the high end of the scale to shy and fearful at the low end, but by and large the Basset temperament is and should be confident and friendly.

If you are fortunate enough to have children in the household or living nearby, your socialization task will be assisted considerably. Basset Hounds raised with well-supervised children are the best. The two seem to understand each other and in some way known only to the puppies and children themselves, they give each other the confidence to face the trying ordeal of growing up.

The children in your own household are not the only children your puppy should spend time with. It is a case of the more the merrier! Every

*Introduce your Basset Hound to different people, especially children. The more people he meets, the better socialized he becomes.*

child (and adult for that matter) who enters your household should be introduced to your Basset Hound. If trustworthy neighbor children live nearby have them come in and spend time with your puppy if there is adult supervision. The children must understand however, that puppies are babies and cannot endure rough handling, nor can they play for hours on end.

Weather permitting, your puppy should go everywhere with you—the post office, the market, the shopping mall—wherever. Be prepared to create a stir wherever you go because the very reason that attracted you to the first Basset Hound you met applies other people as well. Everyone will want to pet your little "sad sack" and there is nothing in the world better for him. An important note, however: *Do not leave your Basset alone in a car during hot or even warm weather!* Temperatures inside a closed car can soar in just a few minutes and this could cause the death of your dog.

The young Basset will quickly learn that all humans—young and old, short and tall, and of all races are friends. You are in charge. You must call the shots.

If your Basset has a show career in his future, there are other things in addition to just being handled that will have to be taught. All Basset show dogs must learn to have their mouth inspected by the judge. The judge must also be able to check the teeth. Males must be accustomed to having their testicles touched as the dog show judge must determine that all male dogs are "complete." This means there are two normal sized testicles in the scrotum. These inspections must begin in puppyhood and be done on a regular and continuing basis.

## THE ADOLESCENT BASSET HOUND

Basset Hounds mature very slowly. While some breeds are mature at 12 months and most at 24 months, the Basset is fast approaching three years of age before most consider it finished with all those "stages." Some lines, however, may mature a bit earlier.

Bassets go through growth periods in "spurts." Parts of the anatomy seem to develop independently of each other. Despair not. Eventually—your Basset will undoubtedly revert back to what it gave promise of being as a puppy.

If a Basset begins to emit an odor, check those long velvety ears or the mouth. Because of lack of air circulation inside the ear, the opening to the ear canal can be a place to harbor ear mites or for infections to start. It may be necessary for your veterinarian to use a swab and do a microscopic examination of the residue inside your dog's ears in order to determine what the problem is.

Your veterinarian can recommend various products to assist you in keeping your Basset's ears clean and odor-free. There is a product for the ears we particularly like that smells like eucalyptus. Putting those ears up in a snood while your Basset is eating can keep the ears out of the food dish and avoid hygiene problems.

The Basset's pendulous lips keep the mouth covered and food can accumulate between the outsides of the teeth and the lips. Check your dog's mouth frequently to make sure the teeth and gums are clean. Allowing your dog to chew on very large knuckle bones can assist keeping the mouth clean, and the use of a tooth brush can assist you with this problem as well. Just remember that although the Basset Hound is shorthaired, the coat requires care and attention.

Food needs change during this growth period. Think of Basset puppies as individualistic as children and act accordingly.

*Children make great playmates for energetic puppies and caring for a dog teaches a child responsibility.*

The amount of food you give your Basset Hound should be adjusted to how much he will consume at each meal and how that amount relates to optimum weight. Most Basset Hounds are good eaters and you must be extremely careful not to let them get too fat. Bassets will give you that forlorn look that says they are at starvation's doorstep regardless of how much food you give them. Excess weight for Basset Hounds (or their owners for that matter!) can be lethal. If the entire meal is eaten quickly, add a small amount to the next feeding and continue to do so as the need increases. This method will ensure you give your puppy enough food, but you must also pay close attention to your dog's appearance.

At eight weeks of age a Basset puppy is eating four meals a day. By the time it is six months old the puppy can do well on two meals a day with perhaps a snack in the middle of the day. If your puppy does not eat the food offered, it is either not hungry or not well. Your dog will eat when it is hungry. If you suspect the dog is not well, a trip to the veterinarian is in order.

Bassets are hounds and have an inbred howling mechanism that they do not hesitate to use—especially when left "home alone." Constant correction and not permitting your young

*Good nutrition will be evident in your dog's healthy appearance and enthusiastic attitude.*

Basset to become accustomed to howling away your absence will certainly be appreciated by your neighbors!

Another hound characteristic is the Basset's trailing ability. The breed is constantly checking the ground for interesting odors to follow and if not kept in a fenced yard, will more likely than not wind up the day's trailing several counties away. Unfortunately Bassets are not blessed with the "homing" instinct of some other breeds. Responsible owners make sure their Basset is kept in a safe and secure environment.

This adolescent period is a particularly important one as it is the time your Basset must learn all the household and social rules by which it live for the rest of its life. Your patience and commitment during this time will not only produce a respected canine good citizen but will forge a bond between the two of you that will grow and ripen into a wonderful relationship.

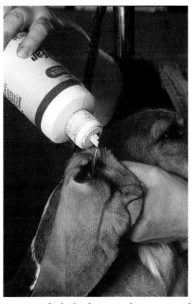

*Because of a lack of air circulation around the Basset's long ears, his ear canal can be prone to infections. Be sure to keep ears clean and free of waxy build-up.*

# CARING for Your Basset Hound

## FEEDING AND NUTRITION

The best way to make sure your Basset puppy is obtaining the right amount and the correct type of food for his age is to follow the diet sheet provided by the breeder from whom you obtain your puppy. Do your best not to change the puppy's diet and you will be less apt to run into digestive problems and diarrhea. Diarrhea is very serious in young puppies. Puppies with diarrhea can dehydrate very rapidly causing severe problems and even death.

If it is necessary to change your Basset puppy's diet for any reason it should be done gradually, over a period of several meals and a few days. Begin by adding a few tablespoons of the new food, gradually increasing the amount until the meal consists entirely of the new product.

By the time your Basset is 10 to 12 months old you can reduce feedings to one or, at the most, twice a day. The main meal can be

*Pick a good-quality dog food that is nutritionally adequate and appropriate for your Basset Hound's stage of life.*

*You must teach your Basset Hound good manners, especially around mealtime. This croissant snatcher is owned by Marsha Jacobs.*

given either in the morning or evening; this is really a matter of choice on your part. There are two important things to remember: Feed the main meal or meals at the same time every day and make sure what you feed is nutritionally complete.

The single meal can be supplemented by a morning or nighttime snack of hard dog biscuits made especially for large dogs. These biscuits not only become highly anticipated treats but are genuinely helpful in maintaining healthy gums and teeth.

**"Balanced" Diets:** In order for a canine diet to qualify as "complete and balanced" in the United States, it must meet standards set by the Subcommittee on Canine Nutrition of the National Research Council of the National Academy of Sciences. Most commercial foods manufactured for dogs meet these standards and prove this by listing the ingredients contained in the food on every package or can. The ingredients are listed in descending order with the main ingredient listed first.

Fed with any regularity at all, refined sugars can quickly cause your Basset to become obese and will definitely create tooth decay. Candy stores do not exist in nature and canine teeth are not genetically disposed to handling sugars. Do not feed your Basset

*When is a Basset Hound most apt to be hungry? When he is awake! This red and white pair are no exception as they attempt to lick their platters clean.*

Hound candy or sweets, and avoid products that contain sugar to any high degree.

Fresh water and a properly prepared, balanced diet containing the essential nutrients in correct proportions are all a healthy Basset Hound needs. Dog foods come canned, dry, semi-moist, "scientifically fortified" and "all-natural." A visit to your local supermarket or pet store will reveal how vast an array you will be able to select from.

All dogs, whether toy or giant, are carnivorous (meat-eating) animals, and the basis for the diet they are fed should be in animal protein. The product can be canned or dried, but check ingredients to make sure that the major ingredient (appearing first on the ingredients list) is in fact animal protein.

Wild carnivores eat the entire beast they capture and kill. The carnivore's kills consist almost entirely of herbivorous (plant-eating) animals, and invariably the carnivore begins its meal with the contents of the herbivore's stomach. This provides the carbohydrates, minerals and nutrients present in vegetables.

Through centuries of domestication we have made our dogs entirely dependent upon us for their well-being. Therefore, we are entirely responsible for duplicating the food balance the wild dog finds in nature. The domesticated dog's diet must include some protein, carbohydrates, fats, roughage and small amounts of essential minerals and vitamins.

Finding commercially prepared diets that contain all the necessary nutrients in the proper balance will not present a problem. It is important to understand, though, that these commercially prepared foods do contain most of the nutrients your Basset Hound requires. Most Basset Hound breeders recommend some vitamin supplementation for healthy coat and increased stamina, especially for showdogs, pregnant bitches or growing puppies.

**Oversupplementation:** A great deal of controversy exists today regarding the orthopedic problems that afflict many breeds. Some claim these problems are entirely hereditary conditions, but many others feel they can be exacerbated by over-use of mineral and vitamin supplements for puppies. Over-supplementation is now looked upon by some breeders as a major contributor to many skeletal abnormalities found in the purebred dogs of the day. In giving vitamin supplementation one should *never* exceed the prescribed amount. No vitamin, however, is a substitute for a nutritious, balanced diet.

Pregnant and lactating bitches do require supplementation of some kind, but here again it is not a case of "if a little is good, a lot

*As Bassets age, they are inclined to become less active. However, even the elderly statesman will benefit from moderate daily exercise.*

would be a great deal better." Extreme caution is advised in this case and best discussed with your veterinarian.

Table scraps should be given only as part of the dog's meal and never from the table. A Basset Hound who becomes accustomed to being hand-fed from the table can become a real pest at mealtime very quickly. Also, dinner guests may find the woeful and pleading stare of your Basset is less than appealing when dinner is being served.

Dogs do not care if food looks like a hot dog or a piece of cheese. Truly nutritious dog foods are seldom manufactured to look like food that appeals to humans. Dogs only care about how food smells and tastes. It is highly doubtful you will be eating your dog's food, so do not waste your money on these "looks just like" products.

**Special Diets:** There are now any number of commercially prepared diets for dogs with special dietary needs. The overweight, underweight or geriatric dog can have its nutritional needs met, as can puppies and growing dogs. The calorie content of these foods is adjusted accordingly. With the correct amount of the right foods and the proper amount of exercise, your Basset should stay in top shape. Again, common sense must prevail. Too many calories will increase weight, too few will reduce weight.

Occasionally a young Basset going through the teething period will become a poor eater. The concerned owner's first response is

*The only thing a Basset Hound enjoys more than the chase is pursuing the prey as part of the pack. This field quintet is owned by William M. Stevens.*

to tempt the dog by hand-feeding special treats and foods that the problem eater seems to prefer. This practice only serves to compound the problem. Once the dog learns to play the waiting game, it will turn up its nose at anything other than its favorite food, knowing full well what it *wants* to eat will eventually arrive.

Unlike humans, dogs have no suicidal tendencies. A healthy dog will not starve

*Every Basset should have his own little corner or space to retire to when he needs to get away. This sleeping beauty is owned by Guillermo and Laura Borda.*

himself to death. He may not eat enough to keep him in the shape we find ideal and attractive but he will definitely eat enough to maintain himself. If your Basset is not eating properly and appears to be too thin, it is probably best to consult your veterinarian.

## SPECIAL NEEDS OF THE BASSET HOUND

### Exercise

Within reason, most anything you can do, your Basset Hound can do, too. Long morning walks, hikes over mountain trails, exploring tide pools along the beach—your Basset will enjoy and benefit from these activities as much as you will.

On the other hand, if your own exercise proclivities lie closer to a good long walk downtown, your Basset can be just as satisfied. While the Basset has an outstanding level of endurance, the breed is not one that has to be worn down before it will lie down. Actually the opposite is true. Given its "druthers," a Basset might well choose to be a couch potato over preparing for the decathlon.

If your Basset shares its life with young children or other dogs, it could be getting enough exercise. The Basset is always ready for a romp or to invent some new game that his best pal or kennelmate might invent.

Slow, steady exercise is best for your Basset—exercise that keeps his heart rate in the working area will do nothing but extend his life. If your Basset is doing all this with you at his side, you are increasing the chances that the two of you will enjoy each other's company for many more years to come.

### Toys and Chewing

Bassets, even as puppies, have great jaw strength for their size and can be very destructive during their teething period. It is said a Basset puppy is part private investigator and part vacuum cleaner. They find things that have yet to be lost and feel everything they find should be stored in their tummies.

"Puppy proofing" your home is a must. Your Basset will be ingenious in getting into things he shouldn't, so you have to be far more clever and keep ahead of what your puppy might get himself into.

Provide toys that will keep the puppy busy and eliminate his need for eating your needlepoint pillow or the legs off your Chippendale table. Just be sure to provide things that are hard to chew up, such as the original *Nylabone®*. Nor should you give a Basset meat bones unless they are the huge beef knuckle bones. Bassets can chew up and shatter most of the smaller bones and may get a perforated or compacted intestine from it.

Never give your puppy old shoes to play with. Dogs can see no difference between an old sneaker you have given them and your

*Good oral care is important to your dog's health and well-being.*

*Take your Basset Hound with you wherever you go! The breed is happiest when allowed to be with the ones he loves.*

brand new Bruno Maglies. Once you've worn shoes, they all smell *exactly* alike to your Basset—age and cost notwithstanding!

## Socialization

The Basset Hound is by nature a happy dog and takes most situations in stride, but it is important to accommodate the breed's natural instincts by making sure your dog is accustomed to everyday events of all kinds. Traffic, strange noises, loud or hyperactive children and strange animals can be very intimidating to a dog of any breed that has never experienced them before. Gently and gradually introduce your puppy to as many strange situations as you possibly can.

Make it a practice to take your Basset with you everywhere whenever practical. The breed is a real crowd pleaser and you will find your dog will savor all the attention it gets.

## BATHING AND GROOMING

Although the Basset Hound does not not have a long coat to

contend with, the breed is no less in need of grooming. The folds and pendulous skin of Bassets can become irritated very easily if not kept clean and dry. Unscented "baby wipes" are excellent for this job. If there is any irritation, this needs to be treated with an ointment that can be obtained from your veterinarian.

This is the time to check the skin thoroughly for any abrasions or cysts. The latter, known as epidermoid cysts, can be found on or just under the skin. It is a problem not uncommon to Basset Hounds, particularly older dogs, and should be brought to the attention of your veterinarian when discovered.

**Nail Trimming:** This is a good time to accustom your Basset Hound to having his nails trimmed and his feet inspected. The Basset's nails are often dark and it is extremely difficult to see the blood vessel running through the center of the nail and into the "quick." The quick grows close to the end of the nail and contains very sensitive nerve endings. If the nail is allowed to grow too long it will be impossible to cut it back to a proper length without cutting into the quick. This causes severe pain to the dog and can also result in a great deal of bleeding that can be very difficult to stop.

The nails of a Basset Hound who spends most of his time indoors or on grass when outdoors can grow long very quickly. Do not allow the nails to become overgrown and then expect to cut them back

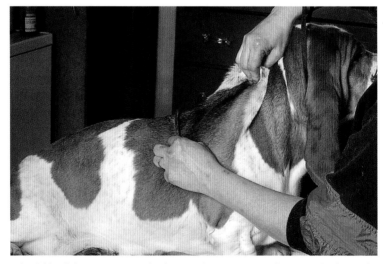

*The folds of the Basset Hound's skin can become irritated very easily if your dog is not kept clean, brushed, and dry.*

*Your Basset Hound is more vulnerable to coat problems like thorns, burrs and parasites when out in the field. Texas-born Petunia poses dutifully in the bluebonnets.*

easily. If your Basset is getting plenty of exercise on cement or rough, hard pavement, the nails may keep sufficiently worn down. Otherwise the nails can grow long very quickly. They must then be carefully trimmed back.

Should the quick be nipped in the trimming process, there are any number of blood clotting products available at pet shops that will almost immediately stem the flow of blood. It is wise to have one of these products on hand in case there is a nail-trimming accident or the dog tears a nail on his own.

There are coarse metal files available at your pet emporium or hardware store that can be used in place of the nail clippers. This is a more gradual method of taking the nail back and one that is far less apt to injure the quick.

Always inspect your dog's feet for cracked pads. Check between the toes for splinters and thorns. Pay particular attention to any swollen or tender areas. In many sections of the country there is a weed that releases a small barbed hook-like affair that carries its seed. This hook easily finds its way into a Basset's foot or between his toes and very quickly works its way deep into the dog's flesh. This will very quickly cause soreness and infection. These barbs

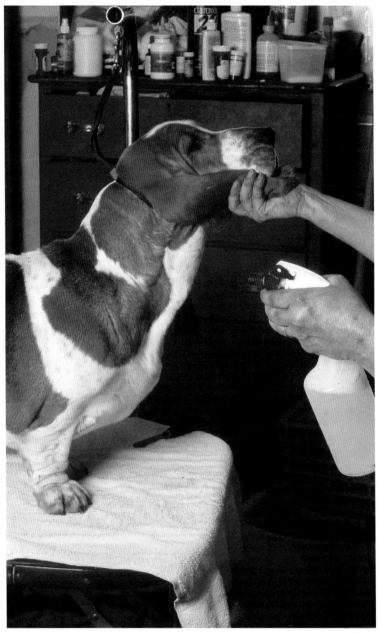

*Bathing your Basset Hound should seldom be necessary as long as you brush him regularly. A spray or damp cloth is useful for removing dirt from your Basset's coat.*

*A Basset Hound competing in conformation must be perfectly groomed.*

should be removed by your veterinarian before serious problems result.

**Bathing:** If brushing is attended to regularly, bathing will seldom be necessary unless your Basset finds his way into something that leaves his coat with a disagreeable odor. Even then, there are many products, both dry and liquid, available at your local pet store that eliminate odors and leave the coat shiny and clean. A damp wash cloth will put the Basset that has given himself a mud bath back in shape very quickly.

Brushing should always be done in the same direction as the hair grows. You should begin at the dog's head brushing toward the tail and down the sides and legs. This procedure will loosen the dead hair and brush it off the dog.

Check the skin inside the thighs and armpits to see if it is dry or red. Artificial heat during winter months can dry out the skin and cause it to become chapped. Place a small amount of petrolium jelly or baby oil on the palms of your hands and rub your hands over the dry areas.

# HOUSETRAINING and Basic Training

Tﾟhere is no breed of dog that cannot be trained. Some breeds appear to be more difficult to get the desired response from than others. Bassets are certainly a case in point. However, this is more apt to be due to the trainer not being "Basset specific" in his or her approach to the training than the dog's inability to learn.

In their innate wisdom, those who created the Basset wanted a dog who would not be dissuaded from the task at hand—trailing the game. This is all well and good except that this tenacity applies to everything the Basset is and does. It takes effort and patience on the part of the trainer to change the Basset Hound's mind. As we have already indicated, the Basset Hound is *not* for the faint of heart.

Ease of training any dog of any breed depends in a great part upon just how much a dog depends upon its master's approval. The entirely dependent dog lives to please its master and will do everything in its power to evoke the approval response from the person it is devoted to. At the opposite end of the pole we have the totally in-dependent dog who is not remotely concerned with what its master thinks. Successfully training a Basset depends upon your fully understanding the breed's character and dealing with it accordingly.

The key to having a well-trained Basset Hound is to start as a very young puppy with play training. While it may be difficult to remind ourselves that our

*Although training your Basset Hound may not always go "by the book," patience and persistence on your part will soon be rewarded.*

*Do not allow your Basset Hound to establish habits you later decide are unacceptable, like sitting on the furniture. Thurston looks like he's not moving for anyone!*

wonderful Bassets trace back to the wolf, doing so will help in understanding our dogs. The wolf mother plays with her cubs and part of that play results in teaching the cubs what they may and may not do. The Basset puppy, like his wolf-cub ancestor, must think he is having fun and has decided on his own to do what he is participating in. If you try to force a Basset to do something, or to stop doing something he is accustomed to doing, before he is ready, you will have your patience tested to the outer limits. Do not allow your "cute little Basset puppy" to do something that you would not want a 60- or 70-pound adult to do.

A puppy's biting your hands or feet, refusing to give up a toy or jumping on you—or on furniture—may appear cute and funny. Your allowing a puppy to do this encourages the behavior, and he will continue to do this into adulthood, which will be far from cute and funny and extremely difficult to stop.

The problem with battles of will is that the Basset's history of tenacity is then called forth and the dog becomes an immovable object. When this immovable object (the Basset) meets the irresistible force (its owner) well, little more need be said!

This is not to say there are to be no rules or regulations in Basset Hound training. On the contrary, it is very important in training

*Make sure your Basset Hound has plenty of time to eliminate outside during the housetraining process.*

a Basset that the dog is absolutely confident of his place in the "pack," which is the human or humans the dog lives with. The Basset's place in the pecking order must be below every family member, and this must be clear to the dog from the first day he enters his new home.

All this is not to indicate the Basset will avoid complying with a surly or aggressive attitude. Not at all. The Basset is more apt to be unconcerned or act as though he never in his life heard about the rule you are trying to enforce.

## HOUSETRAINING

Without a doubt the best way to housebreak a Basset Hound is to use the crate method. First-time dog owners are inclined to initially see the crate method of housebreaking as cruel, but those same people will return later and thank us profusely for having suggested it in the first place. All dogs need a place of their own to retreat to, and you will find the Basset Hound will consider his crate that place.

Use of a crate reduces housetraining time down to an absolute minimum and avoids keeping a puppy under constant stress by incessantly correcting him for making mistakes in the house. The anti-crate advocates consider it cruel to confine a puppy for any length of time but find no problem in constantly harassing and punishing the puppy because it has wet on the carpet and relieved itself behind the sofa.

The crate used for housebreaking should only be large enough for the puppy to stand up and lie down in and stretch out comfortably. These crates are available at most pet emporiums at a wide range of prices. Ideal for Bassets are the fiberglass airline-type crates in the number 300 or 400 size. This size will be larger than what is needed for the very young puppy but it is not necessary to dash out and buy a new cage every few weeks to accommodate your Basset's rapid spurts of growth. Simply cut a piece of plywood of a size to partition off the excess space in the very large cage and move it back as needed.

Begin using the crate to feed your puppy in. Keep the door closed and latched while the puppy is eating. When the meal is finished, open the cage and carry the puppy outdoors to the spot where you want him to learn to eliminate. As you are doing so, you should consistently use the same words. Whether the words are "go out," "potty" or whatever, it makes no difference. The important point is the puppy will be learning both where to eliminate and that certain words mean something is expected.

*These Bassets from Morningwood Kennels look sweet as pie, but are full of boundless energy and mischief.*

In the event you do not have outdoor access or will be away from home for long periods of time, begin housebreaking by placing newspapers in some out-of-the-way corner that is easily accessible for the puppy. If you consistently take your puppy to the same spot you will reinforce the habit of going there for that purpose.

It is important that you do not let the puppy loose after eating. Young puppies will eliminate almost immediately after eating or drinking. They will also be ready to relieve themselves when they first wake up and after playing. If you keep a watchful eye on your puppy you will quickly learn when this is about to take place. A puppy usually circles and sniffs the floor just before it will relieve itself. Do not give your puppy an opportunity to learn that it can eliminate in the house! Your housetraining chores will be reduced considerably if you avoid bad habits in the first place.

If you are not able to watch your puppy every minute, he should be in his crate with the door securely latched. Each time you put your puppy in the crate give him a small treat of some kind. Throw the treat to the back of the crate and encourage the puppy to walk in on his own. When it does so, praise the puppy and perhaps hand him another piece of the treat through the wires of the cage.

Do not succumb to your puppy's complaints about being in its cage. The puppy must learn to stay in his crate and to do so without unnecessary complaining. A quick "No" command and a tap on the crate will usually get the puppy to understand theatrics will not result in liberation.

Do understand a puppy of 8 to 12 weeks will not be able to contain himself for long periods of time. Puppies of that age must relieve themselves every few hours except at night. Your schedule must be adjusted accordingly. Also make sure your puppy has relieved both his bowel and bladder the last thing at night and do not dawdle when you wake up in the morning.

Your first priority in the morning is to get the puppy outdoors. Just how early this ritual will take place will depend much more upon your puppy than upon you. If your Basset Hound is like most others there will be no doubt in your mind when he needs to be let out. You will also very quickly learn to tell the difference between the "this is an emergency" complaint and the "I just want out" grumbling. Do not test the young puppy's ability to contain himself. His vocal demand to be let out is confirmation that the housebreaking lesson is being learned.

Should you find it necessary to be away from home all day you will not be able to leave your puppy in a crate; on the other hand, do not make the mistake of allowing him to roam the house or even a large room at will. Confine the puppy to a small room or partitioned-off area and cover the floor with newspaper. Make this area large enough so that the puppy will not have to relieve himself next to his bed, food or water bowls. You will soon find the puppy will be inclined to use one particular spot to perform his bowel and bladder functions. When you are home you must take the puppy to this exact spot to eliminate at the appropriate time.

## BASIC TRAINING

Early "puppy kindergarten" along with puppy play training are vital if you plan to do obedience work of any kind. While a Basset is as a rule not the easiest dog in the world to train, the AKC annually records a significant number of Bassets that have achieved

*The well-mannered Basset Hound in his natural environment is always a beautiful sight to behold. Fred is both a happy hunter and treasured companion of Marit Jenssen.*

obedience titles. It can be done! There are several titles that can be earned. The requirements for each can be obtained by writing the AKC and requesting their free booklet titled *Obedience Regulations.*

The Companion Dog (CD) title is the least difficult to obtain. This level deals with the basics every Basset Hound should be schooled in: sit, stay, down and heeling on and off leash. One might compare the title to obtaining a bachelors degree.

The Companion Dog Excellent (CDX) title is the next most difficult. This would be comparable to our masters degree This level requires the dog to perform many of the same exercises it did to obtain the CD title but on a more sophisticated level. It also includes jumping obstacles and retrieving.

The more advanced degrees build upon what has been previously required but adds scenting exercises as well. The Utility Dog (UD) title would be like our having completed a doctorate degree. Because of its acute scenting ability, the Basset Hound excels in Tracking and many of them have a Tracking Dog (TD) as well as a Tracking Dog Excellent (TDX) degree.

Most Bassets could probably get their Companion Dog (CD) titles if their owner had patience to live through it all. A Basset's trainer has to understand how the breed sees life. How things are now is just fine with a Basset Hound. Why fix something if it's not broken? Therefore, the Basset Hound has to think about all

*Make sure your Basset Hound puppy has ample time outside. The more opportunity your puppy has to go outside to relieve himself, the less accidents will occur in your home.*

*Never underestimate the athletic ability of the Basset Hound. The breed is much more versatile than people imagine.*

those new "rules" for a good long time before deciding whether they "fit."

The average Basset will not see a good reason to jump an obedience trial's bar or solid jump when the dog can simply walk under or around it more easily.

Why stand when you can sit? Why sit when it's more comfortable to lie down on your back? The human trainer has to be absolutely dedicated, have a good sense of humor and the patience of Job.

Where you are emotionally and the environment in which you train are just as important to your dog's training as is his state of mind at the time. Never begin training when you are irritated, distressed or preoccupied. Nor should

*With the basic "ABCs" of training, your Basset can accomplish anything!*

you begin basic training in a place that interferes with you or your dog's concentration. Once the commands are understood and learned you can begin testing your dog in public places, but at first the two of you should work in a place where you can concentrate fully upon each other.

### The "No!" Command

There is no doubt whatsoever one of the most important commands your Basset puppy will ever learn is the meaning of the "No!" command. It is critical that the puppy learn this command just as soon as possible. One important piece of advice in using this and all other commands—*never give a command you are not prepared and able to follow through on!* The only way a puppy learns to obey commands is to realize that once issued, commands must be complied with. Learning the "no" command should start on the first day of the puppy's arrival at your home.

### Leash Training

It is never too early to accustom the Basset puppy to a collar and leash. It is your way of keeping your dog under control. It may not be necessary for the puppy or adult Basset to wear its collar and

*All Bassets must be leash trained, not only for their safety, but for the safety of others as well.*

*When attempting to housebreak a Basset, your dog should be confined to a relatively small area like the kitchen. Murphy now has full run of the house.*

identification tags within the confines of your home, but no Basset should ever leave home without a collar and without the leash held securely in your hand.

Begin getting your Basset puppy accustomed to his collar by leaving it on for a few minutes at a time. Gradually extend the time you leave the collar on. Most Bassets become accustomed to their collar very quickly and forget they are even wearing one.

Once this is accomplished, attach a lightweight leash to the collar while you are playing with the puppy. Do not try to guide the puppy at first. The point here is to accustom the puppy to the feeling of having something attached to the collar.

Some Basset puppies adapt to their collar very quickly and without any undo resistance learn to be guided with the leash. Other Basset puppies may be absolutely adamant that they will not have any part of leash training and seem intent on strangling themselves before submitting.

Should your puppy be one of the latter, do not force the issue. Simply create a "lasso" with your leash and put your Basset's head and front legs through the lasso opening so that the leash encircles the puppy's shoulders and chest, just behind the front legs. Young Bassets seem to object less to this method than having the leash around their neck.

Encourage your puppy to follow you as you move away. Should the puppy be reluctant to cooperate, coax it along with a treat of some kind. Hold the treat in front of the puppy's nose to encourage him to follow you. Just as soon as the puppy takes a few steps toward

*Obedience classes are a great way for you and your Basset Hound to begin proper training techniques.*

you, praise him enthusiastically and continue to do so as you move along.

Make the initial sessions very brief and very enjoyable. Continue the lessons in your home or yard until the puppy is completely unconcerned about the fact that he is on a leash. With a treat in one hand and the leash in the other you can begin to use both to guide the puppy in the direction you wish to go.

Once the leash around the body is taken in stride and

*Your Basset pup will look to you, his owner, for the discipline he needs to become a well-trained adult.*

the puppy has become accustomed to walking along with you, you can start attaching the leash to your puppy's collar. Your walks can begin in front of the house and eventually extend down the street and eventually around the block. This is one lesson no puppy is too young to learn.

### The "Come" Command

The next most important lesson for the Basset puppy to learn is to come when called, therefore it is very important that the puppy learn his name as soon as possible. Constant repetition is what does the trick in teaching a puppy his name. Use the name every time you talk to your puppy.

Learning to "come" on command could save your Basset's life when the two of you venture out into the world. "Come" is the command a dog must understand has to be obeyed without question, but the dog should not associate that command with fear. Your dog's response to his name and the word "come" should always be associated with a pleasant experience, such as great praise and petting or, particularly in the case of the Basset, a food treat.

When training a Basset it is far easier to avoid the establishment of bad habits than it is to correct them once set. *Never* give the "come" command unless you are sure your Basset puppy will come to you. The very young puppy is far more inclined to respond to learning the "come" command than the older Basset. Use the command initially when the puppy is already on his way to you or give the command while walking or running away from the youngster. Clap your hands and sound very happy and excited about having the puppy join in on this "game."

The very young Basset will normally want to stay as close to his owner as possible, especially in strange surroundings. When your puppy sees you moving away, his natural inclination will be to get close to you. This is a perfect time to use the "come" command.

Later, as the puppy grows more independent and more headstrong (as you now know a Basset is capable of), you may want to attach a long leash or rope to the puppy's collar to ensure the correct response. Do not chase or punish your puppy for not obeying the "come" command. Doing so in the initial stages of training makes the youngster associate the command with something to resist, and this will result in avoidance rather than the immediate positive response you desire. It is imperative that you praise your Basset puppy and give him a treat when he does come to you, even if he voluntarily delays responding for many minutes.

### The "Sit" and "Stay" Commands

Just as important to your Basset's safety (and your sanity!) as the "no!" command and learning to come when called are the "sit" and "stay" commands. Even very young Bassets can learn the sit command

*A Basset Hound is able to participate in everything his owner does, including celebrating the holidays. Humphrey uses his "sit" to pose for a Fourth of July photo.*

*If you are a patient and flexible teacher, your Basset Hound will soon be able to master even the most difficult tasks.*

quickly, especially if the training appears to be a game and a food treat is involved.

First, remember the Basset-in-training should always be on collar and leash for all his lessons. A Basset is certainly not beyond getting up and walking away when he has decided something across the yard is far more interesting than your lessons!

Give the "sit" command immediately before pushing down on your Basset's hindquarters. Praise the dog lavishly when he does sit, even though it is you who made the action take place. Again, a food treat always seems to get the lesson across to the learning Basset.

Put your hand lightly on the dog's rear and repeat the "sit" command several times. If your dog makes an attempt to get up, repeat the command yet again while exerting pressure on the chest. Make your Basset stay in this position for increasing lengths of time. Begin with a few seconds and increase the time as lessons progress over the following weeks.

Should your Basset student attempt to get up or to lie down it should be corrected by simply saying, "sit!" in a firm voice. This should be accompanied by returning the dog to the desired position. Once your

Basset has begun to understand the "sit" command, you may able to assume the position by simply putting your hand on the dog's chest and exerting slight backward pressure.

Only when you decide your dog should get up should he be allowed to do so. Do not test the young Basset's patience to the limits. Remember you are dealing with a baby and the attention span of any youngster is relatively short.

When you do decide the dog can get up, call his name, say "OK" and make a big fuss over him. Praise and a food treat are in order every time your Basset responds correctly.

Once your Basset has mastered the "sit" lesson you may start on the "stay" command. With your dog on leash and facing you, give him the command to "sit," then take a step or two back. If your dog attempts to get up to follow, firmly say, "Sit, stay!" While you are saying this raise your hand, palm toward the dog, and again command "Stay!"

Any attempt on your dog's part to get up must be corrected at once, returning him to the sit position and repeating, "Stay!" Once your dog begins to understand what you want, you can gradually increase the distance you step back. With a long leash attached to your dog's collar (even a clothesline will do) start with a few steps and gradually increase the distance to several yards. Your Basset must eventually learn that the "Sit, stay" command must be obeyed no matter how far away you are. Later on, with advanced training, your dog will learn the command is to be obeyed even when you move entirely out of sight.

Avoid calling the dog *to you* at first. This makes the dog overly anxious to get up and come to you. Until your Basset masters the "sit" lesson and is able to remain in the sit position for as long as you dictate, walk back to your dog and say "OK," which is a signal that the command is over. Later, when your dog becomes more reliable in this respect, you can call him to you.

The "Sit, stay" lesson can take considerable time and patience, especially with the Basset puppy, whose attention span will be very short. It is best to keep the "stay" part of the lesson to a minimum until the Basset is at least five or six months old. Everything in a very young Basset's makeup will urge him to follow you wherever you go. Forcing a very young Basset to operate against his natural instincts can be bewildering for the puppy.

### The "Down" Command

Once your Basset has mastered the "sit" and "stay" commands, you may begin work on "down." This is the single-word command for lie down. Use the "down" command *only* when you want the dog to lie down. If you want your Basset to get off your sofa or to stop jumping up on people use the "off" command. Do not interchange these two commands. Doing so will only serve to confuse your dog, and evoking the right response will become next to impossible.

The "down" position is especially useful if you want your Basset to remain in a particular place for a long period of time. A Basset is far more inclined to stay put when he is lying down than when he is sitting. However, lying in the "correct" position may not be as appealing to your Basset as perhaps stretching out on his side or even on his back! Correct obedience performance dictates that your dog lie on his stomach with his front legs stretched out ahead.

Teaching your Basset to obey this command properly may take more time and patience than the previous lessons the two of you have undertaken. It is believed by some animal behaviorists that assuming the "down" position somehow represents submissiveness to the dog. Considering the nature of Bassets, it is easy to understand how this command could prove more difficult for them to comply with. In the end, once the "down" command has become a part of your Basset's repertory, it seems to be more relaxing for the dog, and you will find he seems less inclined to get up and wander off.

*It's just a short way to the ground for a quick nap for this bunny-chasing pair from Norway.*

*My Love Sweet Shirley owned by Karen Currant is a registered therapy dog and is pictured here at her Therapy Dog graduation.*

With your Basset sitting in front of and facing you, hold a treat in your right hand with the excess part of the leash in your left hand. Hold the treat under the dog's nose and slowly bring your hand down to the ground. Your dog will follow the treat with his head and neck. As he does, give the command "down."

An alternative method of getting your Basset headed into the down position is to move around to the dog's right side and as you draw his attention downward with your right hand, slide your left arm under the dog's front legs and gently slide them forward. In the case of a small puppy you will

*Praise and affection are the best training motivators for your Basset Hound.*

undoubtedly have to be on your knees next to the youngster.

As your Basset's forelegs begin to slide out front, keep moving the treat along the ground until the dog's whole body is lying on the ground while you continually repeat "down." Once your dog has assumed the position you desire, give him the treat and a lot of praise. Continue assisting your Basset into the "down" position until he does so on his own. Be firm and be patient.

### The "Heel" Command

In learning to heel, your Basset will walk on your left side with his shoulder next to your leg no matter which direction you might go or how quickly you turn. Teaching your Basset to heel will not only make your daily walks far more enjoyable, it will make a far more tractable companion when the two of you are in crowded or confusing situations. An untrained Basset Hound, even when on a leash, can be more than a handful to control, particularly if you are carrying packages, opening doors or manipulating stairs or elevators. Bassets usually want to be with you wherever you go, so training him to walk along in the correct position is usually not much of a problem.

We have found a link-chain training collar is very useful for the heeling lesson. It provides both quick pressure around the neck and a snapping sound, both of which get the dog's attention. Erroneously referred to as a "choke collar," the link-chain collar used properly will not choke the dog. The pet shop at which you purchase the training collar will be able to show you the proper way to put this collar on your dog.

As you train your Basset puppy to walk along on the leash, you should accustom the youngster to walk on your left side. The leash should cross your body from the dog's collar to your right hand. The excess portion of the leash will be folded into your right hand and your left hand on the leash will be used to make corrections with the leash.

A quick, short jerk on the leash with your left hand will keep your Basset from lunging side to side, pulling ahead or lagging back. As you make a correction give the "heel" command. Always keep the leash slack insolong as your dog maintains the proper position at your side.

If your dog begins to drift away give the leash a sharp jerk and guide the dog back to the correct position and give the "heel" command. *Do not pull on the lead with steady pressure!* What is needed is a sharp but gentle jerking motion to get your Basset's attention. Remember, it is always "jerk and release."

## TRAINING CLASSES

There are actually few limits to what a patient, consistent Basset owner (and the accent is most definitely on *patient* and *consistent!*) can teach his or her dog. While the Basset may not leap to perform the first time you attempt to teach him something new, take heart. Once your Basset Hound has convinced himself all these "silly" things you have taught him to do are, in reality, fun and will result in a lot of praise (and food!) life will be much easier for the both of you.

Don't forget, you are dealing with a breed that is difficult to convince. As much as your Basset loves and adores you, remember everything in his heritage insists that his mind will not be easily changed. Your Basset performs because he has decided he wants to, not because you are *forcing* him to obey. Do not tell your Basset this, but if you are persistent enough in your training your Basset will eventually think the whole thing was his own idea in the first place!

*Most Basset Hounds live in family environments and learn to conform to the rules of the household.*

For advanced obedience work it is wise for the Basset owner to consider local professional assistance. Professional trainers have had long-standing experience in avoiding the pitfalls of obedience training and can help you to avoid them as well.

This training assistance can be obtained in many ways. The strange dogs and new people encountered at training classes are particularly good for your Basset's socialization. There are free-of-charge or inexpensive classes at many parks and recreation facilities, as well as very formal and sometimes very expensive individual lessons with private trainers.

There are also some obedience schools that will take your Basset and train him for you. However, unless your schedule provides no time at all to train your own dog, having someone else train the dog for you would be last on our list of recommendations. The rapport that develops between the owner who has trained his or her Basset to be a pleasant companion and good canine citizen is very special—well worth the time and patience it requires to achieve.

## BASSET HOUND VERSATILITY

Once your Basset Hound has been taught basic manners, there are countless ways that the two of you can participate in enjoyable events. The breed is highly successful in conformation shows and has proven it can also do well in obedience competition—and certainly there is nothing it will enjoy more than field work. Field work can take the form of trials with specific rules and regulations or as companion to the hunter.

*Bassets make wonderful therapy dogs. Bucky, owned by Marsha Jacobs, works with the Pets on Wheels organization in Phoenix, Arizona.*

## Field Trials

Although we no longer require a Basset to chase a bunny out of the woods to help bring home food for the table, there is a thrill to be had in hearing the sound of the Basset baying on the trail. It never has been the job of the Basset to kill the rabbit, only to chase it out into the open for the hunter.

That chase is marvelous exercise for dog and man. There are a few privately owned Basset packs still in existence. Very often the rabbits encountered by the packs know the terrain and routine so well that they make a game of it, knowing every nook and cranny to hide in or hop over. They manage to stay just that far ahead of the pack to keep the hounds going, but never close enough to be caught. The same rabbits are "hunted" many times a season and none are killed! Even the rabbits seem to enjoy participating in the pursuit.

Sanctioned field trials are held either by the Basset Hound Club of America or by a local club approved to do so. Qualifying and successfully competing in these events earns the dogs their Field Championships. The dates of these trials and the regulations that govern them can be obtained by writing to the BHCA. Field Trials are conducted to test the scenting and trailing ability of the Basset Hound and have their own set of rules.

## Canine Good Citizen

Less demanding but certainly a good introduction to more advanced obedience training are the requirements for a Canine Good Citizen certificate. These certificates are earned by a dog passing a ten-part test as designed by the American Kennel Club. These tests include cleanliness and grooming, socialization, obeying simple commands and general tractability. As the name implies, any dog capable of earning the certificate can only be a better friend and companion.

## Therapy Dogs

Basset Hounds can perform an extremely valuable service by visiting homes for the aged, orphanages and hospitals. Bassets love people, and people are always amused by the dogs because of their woeful looks. It is amazing to see how kind and gentle Basset Hounds are with small children and with people who are ill or feeble. It has been proven these visits provide great therapeutic value to the patients.

The well-trained Basset Hound can provide a whole world of activities for the owner. You are only limited by the amount of time you wish to invest in this remarkable breed.

# SPORT of Purebred Dogs

by Judy Iby

Welcome to the exciting and sometimes frustrating sport of dogs. No doubt you are trying to learn more about dogs or you wouldn't be deep into this book. This section covers the basics that may entice you, further your knowledge and help you to understand the dog world. If you decide to give showing, obedience or any other dog activities a try, then I suggest you seek further help from the appropriate source.

Dog showing has been a very popular sport for a long time and has been taken quite seriously by some. Others only enjoy it as a hobby.

The Kennel Club in England was formed in 1859, the American Kennel Club was established in 1884 and the Canadian Kennel Club was formed in 1888. The purpose of these clubs was to register

*Successful showing requires dedication and preparation, but most of all, it should be an enjoyable experience for handlers and dogs alike.*

*This handsome tri-colored Basset Hound, owned by Jackie Conway, takes time out to sniff the daisies.*

purebred dogs and maintain their Stud Books. In the beginning, the concept of registering dogs was not readily accepted. More than 36 million dogs have been enrolled in the AKC Stud Book since its inception in 1888. Presently the kennel clubs not only register dogs but adopt and enforce rules and regulations governing dog shows, obedience trials and field trials. Over the years they have fostered and encouraged interest in the health and welfare of the purebred dog. They routinely donate funds to veterinary research for study on genetic disorders.

Below are the addresses of the kennel clubs in the United States, Great Britain and Canada.

American Kennel Club
260 Madison Avenue
New York, NY 10016
or 5580 Centerview Drive,
Raleigh, NC 27606

The Kennel Club
1 Clarges Street
Picadilly, London, WIY 8AB, England

The Canadian Kennel Club
89 Skyway Avenue
Etobicoke, Ontario, Canada M9W 6R4

Today there are numerous activities that are enjoyable for both the dog and the handler. Some of the activities include conformation showing, obedience competition, tracking, agility, the Canine Good Citizen Certificate, and a wide range of instinct tests that vary from breed to breed. Where you start depends upon your goals which early on may not be readily apparent.

### PUPPY KINDERGARTEN

Every puppy will benefit from this class. PKT is the foundation for all future dog activities from conformation to "couch potatoes." Pet owners should make an effort to attend even if they never expect to show their dog. The class is designed for puppies about three months of age with graduation at approximately five months of age.

*Every puppy can benefit from basic obedience training. These well-behaved fellows are owned by Helen Hurford.*

*The attention and training you give to your Basset puppy can only benefit both of you in the long run.*

All the puppies will be in the same age group and, even though some may be a little unruly, there should not be any real problem. This class will teach the puppy some beginning obedience. As in all obedience classes the owner learns how to train his own dog. The PKT class gives the puppy the opportunity to interact with other puppies in the same age group and exposes him to strangers, which is very important. Some dogs grow up with behavior problems, one of them being fear of strangers. As you can see, there can be much to gain from this class.

There are some basic obedience exercises that every dog should learn. Some of these can be started with puppy kinder-garten.

*Walking on lead is just one of the many things that your Basset Hound must learn.*

## CONFORMATION

Conformation showing is our oldest dog show sport. This type of showing is based on the dog's appearance—that is his structure, movement and attitude. When considering this type of showing, you need to be aware of your breed's standard and be able to evaluate your dog compared to that standard. The breeder of your puppy or other experienced breeders would be good sources for such an evaluation. Puppies can go through lots of changes over a period of time. I always say most puppies start out as promising hopefuls and then after maturing may be disappointing as show candidates. Even so this should not deter them from being excellent pets.

Usually conformation training classes are offered by the local kennel or obedience clubs. These are excellent places for training puppies. The puppy should be able to walk on a lead before entering such a class. Proper ring procedure and technique for posing (stacking) the dog will be demonstrated as well as gaiting the dog. Usually certain patterns are used in the ring such as the triangle or

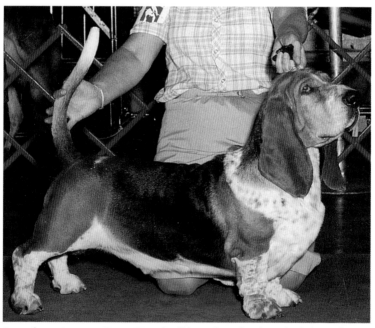

*In conformation, your Basset Hound will be evaluated on how closely he conforms to the standard of the breed.*

the "L." Conformation class, like the PKT class, will give your youngster the opportunity to socialize with different breeds of dogs and humans too.

It takes some time to learn the routine of conformation showing. Usually one starts at the puppy matches which may be AKC Sanctioned or Fun Matches. These matches are generally for puppies from two or three months to a year old, and there may be classes for the adult over the age of 12 months. Similar to point shows, the classes are divided by sex and after completion of the classes in that

*Conformation is just one of the many activities in which you and your Basset Hound can compete.*

breed or variety, the class winners compete for Best of Breed or Variety. The winner goes on to compete in the Group and the Group winners compete for Best in Match. No championship points are awarded for match wins.

A few matches can be great training for puppies even though there is no intention to go on showing. Matches enable the puppy to meet new people and be handled by a stranger—the judge. It is also a change of environment, which broadens the horizon for both dog and handler. Matches and other dog activities boost the confidence of the handler and especially the younger handlers.

Earning an AKC championship is built on a point system, which is different from Great Britain. To become an AKC Champion of Record the dog must earn 15 points. The number of points earned each time depends upon the number of dogs in competition. The number of points available at each show depends upon the breed, its sex and the location of the show. The United States is divided into ten AKC zones. Each zone has its own set of points. The purpose of the zones is to try to equalize the points available from breed to breed and area to area. The AKC adjusts the point scale annually.

The number of points that can be won at a show are between one and five. Three-, four- and five-point wins are considered majors.

Not only does the dog need 15 points won under three different judges, but those points must include two majors under two different judges. Canada also works on a point system but majors are not required.

Dogs always show before bitches. The classes available to those seeking points are: Puppy (which may be divided into 6 to 9 months and 9 to 12 months); 12 to 18 months; Novice; Bred-by-Exhibitor; American-bred; and Open. The class winners of the same sex of each breed or variety compete against each other for Winners Dog and Winners Bitch. A Reserve Winners Dog and Reserve Winners Bitch are also awarded but do not carry any points unless the Winners win is disallowed by AKC. The Winners Dog and Bitch compete with the specials (those dogs that have attained championship) for Best of Breed or Variety, Best of Winners and Best of Opposite Sex. It is possible to pick up an extra point or even a major if the points are higher for the defeated winner than those of Best of Winners. The latter would get the higher total from the defeated winner.

At an all-breed show, each Best of Breed or Variety winner will go on to his respective Group and then the Group winners will compete against each other for Best in Show. There are seven Groups: Sporting, Hounds, Working, Terriers, Toys, Non-Sporting and Herding. Obviously there are no Groups at speciality shows (those shows that have only one breed or a show such as the American Spaniel Club's Flushing Spaniel Show, which is for all flushing spaniel breeds).

Earning a championship in England is somewhat different since they do not have a point system. Challenge Certificates are awarded if the judge feels the dog is deserving regardless of the number of dogs in competition. A dog must earn three Challenge Certificates under three different judges, with at least one of these Certificates being won after the age of 12 months. Competition is very strong and entries may be higher than they are in the U.S. The Kennel Club's Challenge Certificates are only available at Championship Shows.

In England, The Kennel Club regulations require that certain dogs, Border Collies and Gundog breeds, qualify in a working capacity (i.e., obedience or field trials) before becoming a full Champion. If they do not qualify in the working aspect, then they are designated a Show Champion, which is equivalent to the AKC's

Champion of Record. A Gundog may be granted the title of Field Trial Champion (FT Ch.) if it passes all the tests in the field but would also have to qualify in conformation before becoming a full Champion. A Border Collie that earns the title of Obedience Champion (Ob Ch.) must also qualify in the conformation ring before becoming a Champion.

The U.S. doesn't have a designation full Champion but does award for Dual and Triple Champions. The Dual Champion must be a Champion of Record, and either Champion Tracker, Herding Champion, Obedience Trial Champion or Field Champion. Any dog that has been awarded the titles of Champion of Record, and any two of the following: Champion Tracker, Herding Champion, Obedience Trial Champion or Field Champion, may be designated as a Triple Champion.

The shows in England seem to put more emphasis on breeder judges than those in the U.S. There is much competition within the

*While conformation is based on the dog's appearance, no points are awarded for attire.*

breeds. Therefore the quality of the individual breeds should be very good. In the United States we tend to have more "all around judges" (those that judge multiple breeds) and use the breeder judges at the specialty shows. Breeder judges are more familiar with their own breed since they are actively breeding that breed or did so at one time. Americans emphasize Group and Best in Show wins and promote them accordingly.

It is my understanding that the shows in England can be very large and extend over several days, with the Groups being scheduled on different days. In our country we have cluster shows, where several different clubs will use the same show site over consecutive days.

Westminster Kennel Club is our most prestigious show although the entry is limited to 2500. In recent years, entry has been limited to Champions. This show is more formal than the majority of the shows with the judges wearing formal attire and the handlers fashionably dressed. In most instances the quality of the dogs is superb. After all, it is a show of Champions. It is a good show to study the AKC registered breeds and is by far the most exciting—especially since it is televised! WKC is one of the few shows in this country that is still benched. This means the dog must be in his benched area during the show hours except when he is being groomed, in the ring, or being exercised.

Typically, the handlers are very particular about their appearances. They are careful not to wear something that will detract from their dog but will perhaps enhance it. American ring procedure is quite formal compared to that of other countries. I remember being reprimanded by a judge because I made a suggestion to a friend holding my second dog outside the ring. I certainly could have used more discretion so I would not call attention to myself. There is a certain etiquette expected between the judge and exhibitor and among the other exhibitors. Of course it is not always the case but the judge is supposed to be polite, not engaging in small talk or even acknowledging that he knows the handler. I understand that there is a more informal and relaxed atmosphere at the shows in other countries. For instance, the dress code is more casual. I can see where this might be more fun for the exhibitor and especially for the novice. This country is very handler-oriented in many of the breeds. It is true, in most instances, that the experienced professional handler can present the dog better and will have a feel for what a judge likes.

*A shining example of the breed, Ch. Fort Merill Snow Job was bred by the author and is owned by Sr. Ivan Tudor of Rio de Janiero, Brazil.*

In England, Crufts is The Kennel Club's own show and is most assuredly the largest dog show in the world. They've been known to have an entry of nearly 20,000, and the show lasts four days. Entry is only gained by qualifying through winning in specified classes at another Championship Show. Westminster is strictly conformation, but Crufts exhibitors and spectators enjoy not only conformation but obedience, agility and a multitude of exhibitions as well. Obedience was admitted in 1957 and agility in 1983.

If you are handling your own dog, please give some consideration to your apparel. For sure the dress code at matches is more informal than the point shows. However, you should wear something a little more appropriate than beach attire or ragged jeans and bare feet. If you check out the handlers and see what is presently fashionable, you'll catch on. Men usually dress with a shirt and tie and a nice sports coat. Whether you are male or female, you will want to wear comfortable clothes and shoes. You need to be able to run with your dog and you certainly don't want to take a chance of falling and hurting yourself. Heaven forbid, if nothing else, you'll upset your dog. Women usually wear a dress or two-piece outfit, preferably with pockets to carry bait, comb, brush, etc. In this case men are the lucky ones with all their pockets. Ladies, think about where your dress will be if you need to kneel on the floor and also think about running. Does it allow freedom to do so?

You need to take along dog; crate; ex pen (if you use one); extra newspaper; water pail and water; all required grooming equipment, including hair dryer and extension cord; table; chair for you; bait for dog and lunch for you and friends; and, last but not least, clean up materials, such as plastic bags, paper towels, and perhaps a bath towel and some shampoo—just in case. Don't forget your entry confirmation and directions to the show.

If you are showing in obedience, then you will want to wear pants. Many of our top obedience handlers wear pants that are color-coordinated with their dogs. The philosophy is that imperfections in the black dog will be less obvious next to your black pants.

Whether you are showing in conformation, Junior Showmanship or obedience, you need to watch the clock and be sure you are not late. It is customary to pick up your conformation armband a few minutes before the start of the class. They will not wait for you and if you are on the show grounds and not in the ring, you will upset everyone. It's a little more complicated picking up your obedience armband if you show later in the class. If you have not picked up your armband and they get to your number, you may not be allowed to show. It's best to pick up your armband early, but then you may show earlier than expected if other handlers don't pick up. Customarily all conflicts should be discussed with the judge prior to the start of the class.

### Junior Showmanship

The Junior Showmanship Class is a wonderful way to build self confidence even if there are no aspirations of staying with the dog-show game later in life. Frequently, Junior Showmanship becomes the background of those who become successful exhibitors/handlers in the future. In some instances it is taken very seriously, and success is measured in terms of wins. The Junior Handler is judged solely on his ability and skill in presenting his dog. The dog's conformation is not to be considered by the judge. Even so the condition and grooming of the dog may be a reflection upon the handler.

Usually the matches and point shows include different classes. The Junior Handler's dog may be entered in a breed or obedience

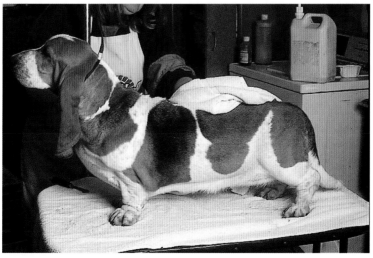

*Your Basset Hound must become accustomed to extensive grooming if he is to be shown in conformation.*

*Handlers should wear comfortable clothing that complements the dog and allows them to move about freely.*

class and even shown by another person in that class. Junior Showmanship classes are usually divided by age and perhaps sex. The age is determined by the handler's age on the day of the show.

## CANINE GOOD CITIZEN®

The AKC sponsors a program to encourage dog owners to train their dogs. Local clubs perform the pass/fail tests, and dogs who pass are awarded a Canine Good Citizen® Certificate. Proof of vaccination is required at the time of participation. The test includes:

1. Accepting a friendly stranger.
2. Sitting politely for petting.
3. Appearance and grooming.
4. Walking on a loose leash.
5. Walking through a crowd.
6. Sit and down on command/staying in place.
7. Come when called.
8. Reaction to another dog.
9. Reactions to distractions.
10. Supervised separation.

If more effort was made by pet owners to accomplish these exercises, fewer dogs would be cast off to the humane shelter.

## OBEDIENCE

Obedience is necessary, without a doubt, but it can also become a wonderful hobby or even an obsession. In my opinion, obedience classes and competition can provide wonderful companionship, not only with your dog but with your classmates or fellow competitors. It is always gratifying to discuss your dog's problems with others who have had similar experiences. The AKC acknowledged Obedience around 1936, and it has changed tremendously even though many of the exercises are basically the same. Today, obedience competition is just that—very competitive. Even so, it is possible for every obedience exhibitor to come home a winner (by earning qualifying scores) even though he/she may not earn a placement in the class.

Most of the obedience titles are awarded after earning three qualifying scores (legs) in the appropriate class under three different judges. These classes offer a perfect score of 200, which is extremely rare. Each of the class exercises has its own point value. A leg is earned after receiving a score of at least 170 and at least 50 percent of the points available in each exercise.

After achieving the UD title, you may feel inclined to go after the UDX and/or OTCh. The UDX (Utility Dog Excellent) title went into effect in January 1994. It is not easily attained. The title

*To become a Canine Good Citizen®, your Basset Hound must be able to get along with people, especially children. This Basset has certainly passed the test!*

requires qualifying simultaneously ten times in Open B and Utility B but not necessarily at consecutive shows.

The OTCh (Obedience Trial Champion) is awarded after the dog has earned his UD and then goes on to earn 100 championship points, a first place in Utility, a first place in Open and another first place in either class. The placements must be won under three different judges at all-breed obedience trials. The points are determined by the number of dogs competing in the Open B and Utility B classes. The OTCh title precedes the dog's name.

Obedience matches (AKC Sanctioned, Fun, and Show and Go) are usually available. Usually they are sponsored by the local obedience clubs. When preparing an obedience dog for a title, you will find matches very helpful. Fun Matches and Show and Go Matches are more lenient in allowing you to make corrections in the ring. I frequently train (correct) in the ring and inform the judge that I would like to do so and to please mark me "exhibition." This means that I will not be eligible for any prize. This type of training is usually very necessary for the Open and Utility Classes. AKC Sanctioned Obedience Matches do not allow corrections in the ring since they must abide by the AKC Obedience Regulations. If you are interested in showing in obedience, then you should contact the AKC for a copy of the Obedience Regulations.

*Who knows how far these sweet little pups can go with the proper training?*

*A Basset Hound will try anything at least once. Dyna, owned by Steve and Alice Steiner, looks like she's enjoying her own private river raft.*

## TRACKING

Tracking is officially classified obedience, but I feel it should have its own category. There are three tracking titles available: Tracking Dog (TD), Tracking Dog Excellent (TDX), Variable Surface Tracking (VST). If all three tracking titles are obtained, then the dog officially becomes a CT (Champion Tracker). The CT will go in front of the dog's name.

A TD may be earned anytime and does not have to follow the other obedience titles. There are many exhibitors that prefer tracking to obedience, and there are others like myself that do both. In my experience with small dogs, I prefer to earn the CD and CDX before attempting tracking. My reasoning is that small dogs are closer to the mat in the obedience rings and therefore it's too easy to put the nose down and sniff. Tracking encourages sniffing. Of course this depends on the dog. I've had some dogs that tracked around the ring and others (TDXs) who wouldn't think of sniffing in the ring.

## AGILITY

Agility was first introduced by John Varley in England at the Crufts Dog Show, February 1978, but Peter Meanwell, competitor and judge, actually developed the idea. It was officially recognized in the early '80s. Agility is extremely popular in England and Canada and growing in popularity in the U.S. The AKC acknowledged agility in August 1994. Dogs must be at least 12 months of age to be entered. It is a fascinating sport that the dog, handler and spectators enjoy to the utmost. Agility is a spectator sport! The dog performs off lead. The handler either runs with his dog or positions himself on the course and directs his dog with verbal and hand signals over a timed course over or through a variety of obstacles including a time out or pause. One of the main drawbacks to agility is finding a place to train. The obstacles take up a lot of space and it is very time consuming to put up and take down courses.

The titles earned at AKC agility trials are Novice Agility Dog (NAD), Open Agility Dog (OAD), Agility Dog Excellent (ADX), and Master Agility Excellent (MAX). In order to acquire an agility title, a dog must earn a qualifying score in its respective class on three separate occasions under two different judges. The MAX will be awarded after earning ten qualifying scores in the Agility Excellent Class.

*Performance tests allow your Basset Hound to do what he instinctively does best—use his nose.*

*Agility allows the Basset Hound to apply his natural athleticism to the competition ring.*

## PERFORMANCE TESTS

During the last decade the American Kennel Club has promoted performance tests—those events that test the different breeds' natural abilities. This type of event encourages a handler to devote even more time to his dog and retain the natural instincts of his breed heritage. It is an important part of the wonderful world of dogs.

## GENERAL INFORMATION

Obedience, tracking and agility allow the purebred dog with an Indefinite Listing Privilege (ILP) number or a limited registration to be exhibited and earn titles. Application must be made to the AKC for an ILP number.

*There are so many activities you and your dog can participate in and the Basset Hound has the ability to excel at them all.*

The American Kennel Club publishes a monthly *Events* magazine that is part of the *Gazette*, their official journal for the sport of purebred dogs. The *Events* section lists upcoming shows and the secretary or superintendent for them. The majority of the conformation shows in the U.S. are overseen by licensed superintendents. Generally the entry closing date is approximately two-and-a-half weeks before the actual show. Point shows are fairly expensive, while the match shows cost about one third of the point show entry fee. Match shows usually take entries the day of the show but some are pre-entry. The best way to find match show information is through your local kennel club. Upon asking, the AKC can provide you with a list of superintendents, and you can write and ask to be put on their mailing lists.

*Showing your Basset Hound takes time, dedication and teamwork, but you and your dog can only benefit from the bond that will form between you.*

Obedience trial and tracking test information is available through the AKC. Frequently these events are not superintended, but put on by the host club. Therefore you would make the entry with the event's secretary.

As you have read, there are numerous activities you can share with your dog. Regardless what you do, it does take teamwork. Your dog can only benefit from your attention and training. I hope this chapter has enlightened you and hope, if nothing else, you will attend a show here and there. Perhaps you will start with a puppy kindergarten class, and who knows where it may lead!

# HEALTH CARE

by Judy Iby

Veterinary medicine has become far more sophisticated than what was available to our ancestors. This can be attributed to the increase in household pets and consequently the demand for better care for them. Also human medicine has become far more complex. Today diagnostic testing in veterinary medicine parallels human diagnostics. Because of better technology we can expect our pets to live healthier lives thereby increasing their life spans.

## THE FIRST CHECK UP

You will want to take your new puppy/dog in for its first check up within 48 to 72 hours after acquiring it. Many breeders strongly recommend this check up and so do the humane shelters. A puppy/dog can appear healthy but it may have a serious problem that is not apparent to the layman. Most pets have some type of a minor flaw that may never cause a real problem.

Unfortunately if he/she should have a serious problem, you will want to consider the consequences of keeping the pet and the attachments that will be formed, which may be broken prematurely. Keep in mind there are many healthy dogs looking for good homes.

This first check up is a good time to establish yourself with the veterinarian and learn the office policy regarding their hours and how they handle emergencies. Usually the breeder or another conscientious pet owner is a good reference for locating a capable veterinarian. You should be aware that not all veterinarians give the same quality of service. Please do not make your selection on the least expensive clinic, as they may be short changing your pet. There is the possibility that eventually it will cost you more due to improper diagnosis, treatment, etc. If you are selecting a new veterinarian, feel free to ask for a tour of the clinic. You should inquire about making an appointment for a tour since all clinics are working clinics, and therefore may not be available all day for sightseers. You may worry less if you see where your pet will be spending the day if he ever needs to be hospitalized.

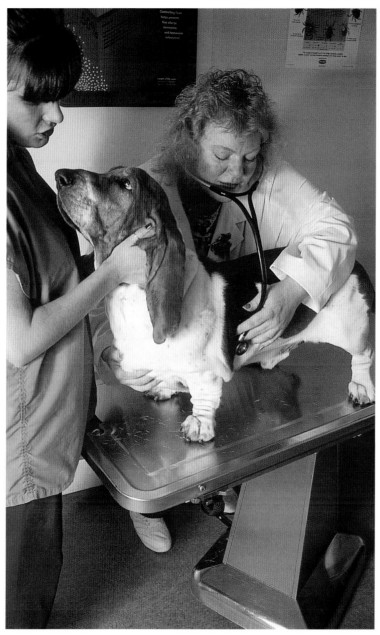

*Your Basset Hound will need regular check-ups to maintain his good health and prevent potential problems.*

## THE PHYSICAL EXAM

Your veterinarian will check your pet's overall condition, which includes listening to the heart; checking the respiration; feeling the abdomen, muscles and joints; checking the mouth, which includes the gum color and signs of gum disease along with plaque buildup; checking the ears for signs of an infection or ear mites; examining the eyes; and, last but not least, checking the condition of the skin and coat.

He should ask you questions regarding your pet's eating and elimination habits and invite you to relay your questions. It is a good idea to prepare a list so as not to forget anything. He should discuss the proper diet and the quantity to be fed. If this should differ from your breeder's recommendation, then you should convey to him the breeder's choice and see if he approves. If he recommends changing the diet, then this should be done over a few days so as not to cause a gastrointestinal upset. It is customary to take in a fresh stool sample (just a small amount) for a test for intestinal parasites. It must be fresh, preferably within 12 hours, since the eggs hatch quickly and after hatching will not be observed under the microscope. If your pet isn't obliging then, usually the technician can take one in the clinic.

*Maternal antibodies protect puppies from disease the first few weeks of life. Vaccinations are needed because the antibodies are only temporarily effective.*

*Basset mothers are calm and loving caretakers. Maggie owned by Joan Urban and her pups are a contented and happy family.*

## IMMUNIZATIONS

It is important that you take your puppy/dog's vaccination record with you on your first visit. In case of a puppy, presumably the breeder has seen to the vaccinations up to the time you acquired custody. Veterinarians differ in their vaccination protocol. It is not unusual for your puppy to have received vaccinations for distemper, hepatitis, leptospirosis, parvovirus and parainfluenza every two to three weeks from the age of five or six weeks. Usually this is a combined injection and is typically called the DHLPP. The DHLPP is given through at least 12 to 14 weeks of age, and it is customary to continue with another parvovirus vaccine at 16 to 18 weeks. You may wonder why so many immunizations are necessary. No one knows for sure when the puppy's maternal antibodies are gone, although it is customarily accepted that distemper antibodies are gone by 12 weeks. Usually parvovirus antibodies are gone by 16 to

18 weeks of age. However, it is possible for the maternal antibodies to be gone at a much earlier age or even a later age. Therefore immunizations are started at an early age. The vaccine will not give immunity as long as there are maternal antibodies.

The rabies vaccination is given at three or six months of age depending on your local laws. A vaccine for bordetella (kennel cough) is advisable and can be given anytime from the age of five weeks. The coronavirus is not commonly given unless there is a problem locally. The Lyme vaccine is necessary in endemic areas. Lyme disease has been reported in 47 states.

### Distemper

This is virtually an incurable disease. If the dog recovers, he is subject to severe nervous disorders. The virus attacks every tissue in the body and resembles a bad cold with a fever. It can cause a runny nose and eyes and cause gastrointestinal disorders, including a poor appetite, vomiting and diarrhea. The virus is carried by raccoons, foxes, wolves, mink and other dogs. Unvaccinated youngsters and senior citizens are very susceptible. This is still a common disease.

*Bordetella attached to canine cilia. Otherwise known as kennel cough, this highly contagious disease should be vaccinated against routinely.*

### Hepatitis

This is a virus that is most serious in very young dogs. It is spread by contact with an infected animal or its stool or urine. The virus affects the liver and kidneys and is characterized by high fever, depression and lack of appetite. Recovered animals may be afflicted with chronic illnesses.

### Leptospirosis

This is a bacterial disease transmitted by contact with the urine of an infected dog, rat or other wildlife. It produces severe symptoms of fever, depression, jaundice and internal bleeding and was fatal before the vaccine was developed. Recovered dogs can be carriers, and the disease can be transmitted from dogs to humans.

### Parvovirus
This was first noted in the late 1970s and is still a fatal disease. However, with proper vaccinations, early

*Your Basset Hound can be subject to fleas and ticks when outside. Check your dog's coat thoroughly for any parasites after playing outdoors.*

diagnosis and prompt treatment, it is a manageable disease. It attacks the bone marrow and intestinal tract. The symptoms include depression, loss of appetite, vomiting, diarrhea and collapse. Immediate medical attention is of the essence.

### Rabies
This is shed in the saliva and is carried by raccoons, skunks, foxes, other dogs and cats. It attacks nerve tissue, resulting in paralysis and death. Rabies can be transmitted to people and is virtually always fatal. This disease is reappearing in the suburbs.

### Bordetella (Kennel Cough)
The symptoms are coughing, sneezing, hacking and retching accompanied by nasal discharge usually lasting from a few days to several weeks. There are several disease-producing organisms responsible for this disease. The present vaccines are helpful but do not protect for all the strains. It usually is not life threatening but in some instances it can progress to a serious bronchopneumonia. The disease is highly contagious. The vaccination should be given routinely for dogs that come in contact with other dogs, such as through boarding, training class or visits to the groomer.

### Coronavirus
This is usually self limiting and not life threatening. It was first noted in the late '70s about a year before parvovirus. The virus

produces a yellow/brown stool and there may be depression, vomiting and diarrhea.

### Lyme Disease

This was first diagnosed in the United States in 1976 in Lyme, CT in people who lived in close proximity to the deer tick. Symptoms may include acute lameness, fever, swelling of joints and loss of appetite. Your veterinarian can advise you if you live in an endemic area.

After your puppy has completed his puppy vaccinations, you will continue to booster the DHLPP once a year. It is customary to booster the rabies one year after the first vaccine and then, depending on where you live, it should be boostered every year or every three years. This depends on your local laws. The Lyme and corona vaccines are boostered annually and it is recommended that the bordetella be boostered every six to eight months.

*Dogs can pick up diseases from other dogs. Make sure your Basset is properly vaccinated before taking him out to make friends. Meet Koko and Chloe, owned by Mike and Lori Pfiefer.*

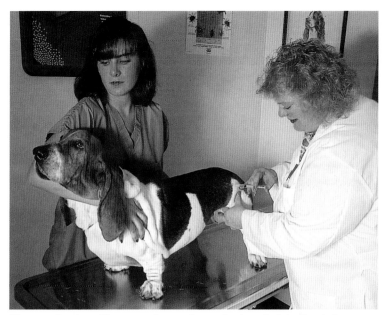

*Your veterinarian will put your dog on a immunization schedule when he is a puppy, and he will then need regular booster shots to prevent disease.*

## ANNUAL VISIT

I would like to impress the importance of the annual check up, which would include the booster vaccinations, check for intestinal parasites and test for heartworm. Today in our very busy world it is rush, rush and see "how much you can get for how little." Unbelievably, some non-veterinary businesses have entered into the vaccination business. More harm than good can come to your dog through improper vaccinations, possibly from inferior vaccines and/or the wrong schedule. More than likely you truly care about your companion dog and over the years you have devoted much time and expense to his well being. Perhaps you are unaware that a vaccination is not just a vaccination. There is more involved. Please, please follow through with regular physical examinations. It is so important for your veterinarian to know your dog and this is especially true during middle age through the geriatric years. More than likely your older dog will require more than one physical a year. The annual physical is good preventive medicine. Through early diagnosis and subsequent treatment your dog can maintain a longer and better quality of life.

## INTESTINAL PARASITES

### Hookworms

These are almost microscopic intestinal worms that can cause anemia and therefore serious problems, including death, in young puppies. Hookworms can be transmitted to humans through penetration of the skin. Puppies may be born with them.

### Roundworms

These are spaghetti-like worms that can cause a potbellied appearance and dull coat along with more severe symptoms, such as vomiting, diarrhea and coughing. Puppies acquire these while in the mother's uterus and through lactation. Both hookworms and roundworms may be acquired through ingestion.

### Whipworms

These have a three-month life cycle and are not acquired through the dam. They cause intermittent diarrhea usually with mucus. Whipworms are possibly the most difficult worm to eradicate. Their eggs are very resistant to most environmental factors and can last for years until the proper conditions enable them to mature. Whipworms are seldom seen in the stool.

Intestinal parasites are more prevalent in some areas than others. Climate, soil and contamination are big factors contributing to the incidence of intestinal parasites. Eggs are passed in the stool, lay on the ground and then become infective in a certain number of days. Each of the above worms has a different life cycle. Your best chance of becoming and remaining worm-free is to always pooper-scoop your yard. A

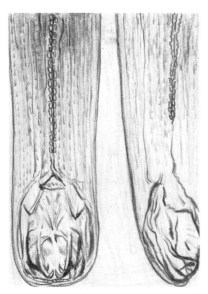

*Hookworms are almost microscopic intestinal worms that can cause anemia and therefore serious problems, even death.*

fenced-in yard keeps stray dogs out, which is certainly helpful.

I would recommend having a fecal examination on your dog twice a year or more often if there is a problem. If your dog has a positive fecal sample, then he will be given the appropriate medication and you will be asked to bring back another stool sample in a certain period of time (depending on the type of worm) and then be rewormed.

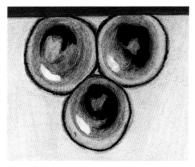

*Roundworm eggs, as would be seen on a fecal evaluation. The eggs must develop for at least 12 days before they are infective.*

This process goes on until he has at least two negative samples. The different types of worms require different medications. You will be wasting your money and doing your dog an injustice by buying over-the-counter medication without first consulting your veterinarian.

## OTHER INTERNAL PARASITES

### Coccidiosis and Giardiasis

These protozoal infections usually affect puppies, especially in places where large numbers of puppies are brought together. Older dogs may harbor these infections but do not show signs unless they are stressed. Symptoms include diarrhea, weight loss and lack of appetite. These infections are not always apparent in the fecal examination.

### Tapeworms

Seldom apparent on fecal floatation, they are diagnosed frequently as rice-like segments around the dog's anus and the base of the tail. Tapeworms are long, flat and ribbon like, sometimes several feet in length, and made up of many segments about five-eighths of an inch long. The two most common types of tapeworms found in the dog are:

(1) First the larval form of the flea tapeworm parasite must mature in an intermediate host, the flea, before it can become infective. Your dog acquires this by ingesting the flea through licking and chewing.

(2) Rabbits, rodents and certain large game animals serve as intermediate hosts for other species of tapeworms. If your dog should eat one of these infected hosts, then he can acquire tapeworms.

## HEARTWORM DISEASE

This is a worm that resides in the heart and adjacent blood vessels of the lung that produces microfilaria, which circulate in the bloodstream. It is possible for a dog to be infected with any number of worms from one to a hundred that can be 6 to 14 inches long. It is a life-threatening disease, expensive to treat and easily prevented. Depending on where you live, your veterinarian may recommend a preventive year-round and either an annual or semiannual blood test. The most common preventive is given once a month.

## EXTERNAL PARASITES

### Fleas

These pests are not only the dog's worst enemy but also enemy to the owner's pocketbook. Preventing is less expensive than treating, but regardless I think we'd prefer to spend our money elsewhere. I would guess that the majority of our dogs are allergic to the bite of a flea, and in many cases it only takes one flea bite. The protein in the flea's saliva is the culprit. Allergic dogs have a reaction, which usually results in a "hot spot." More than likely such a reaction will involve a trip to the veterinarian for treatment. Yes, prevention is less expensive. Fortunately today there are several good products available.

If there is a flea infestation, no one product is going to correct the problem. Not only will the dog require treatment so will the environment. In general flea collars are not very effective although there is now available an "egg" collar that will kill the eggs on the dog. Dips are the most economical but they are messy. There are some effective shampoos and treatments available through pet shops and veterinarians. An oral tablet arrived on the American market in 1995 and was popular in Europe the previous year. It sterilizes the female flea but will not kill adult fleas. Therefore the tablet, which is given monthly, will decrease the flea population but is not a "cure-all." Those dogs that suffer from flea-bite allergy will still be subjected to the bite of the flea. Another popular parasiticide is permethrin, which is applied to the back of the dog in one or two places depending on the dog's weight. This product works as a repellent causing the flea to get "hot feet" and jump off. Do not confuse this product with some of the organophosphates that are also applied to the dog's back.

Some products are not usable on young puppies. Treating fleas should be done under your veterinarian's guidance. Frequently it is necessary to combine products and the layman does not have the knowledge regarding possible toxicities. It is hard to believe but there are a few dogs that do have a natural resistance to fleas. Nevertheless it would be wise to treat all pets at the same time. Don't forget your cats. Cats just love to prowl the neighborhood and consequently return with unwanted guests.

Adult fleas live on the dog but their eggs drop off the dog into the environment. There they go through four larval stages before reaching adulthood, and thereby are able to jump back on the poor unsuspecting dog. The cycle resumes and takes between 21 to 28 days under ideal conditions. There are environmental products available that will kill both the adult fleas and the larvae.

*Because many plants can be poisonous to your dog, always supervise your Basset Hound carefully when outdoors.*

## Ticks

Ticks carry Rocky Mountain Spotted Fever, Lyme disease and can cause tick paralysis. They should be removed with tweezers, trying to pull out the head. The jaws carry disease. There is a tick preventive collar that does an excellent job. The ticks automatically back out on those dogs wearing collars.

## Sarcoptic Mange

This is a mite that is difficult to find on skin scrapings. The pinnal reflex is a good indicator of this disease. Rub the ends of the pinna (ear) together and the dog will start scratching with his foot. Sarcoptes are highly contagious to other dogs and to humans although they do not live long on humans. They cause intense itching.

*Although the Basset can endure all kinds of weather, this forlorn Basset, owned by Jane Wilner, looks as though he can't wait for the sun.*

## Demodectic Mange

This is a mite that is passed from the dam to her puppies. It affects youngsters age three to ten months. Diagnosis is confirmed by skin scraping. Small areas of alopecia around the eyes, lips and/or forelegs become visible. There is little itching unless there is a secondary bacterial infection. Some breeds are afflicted more than others.

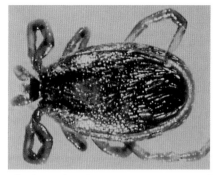

*The deer tick is the most common carrier of Lyme disease. Photo courtesy of Virbac Laboratories, Inc., Fort Worth, Texas.*

## Cheyletiella

This causes intense itching and is diagnosed by skin scraping. It lives in the outer layers of the skin of dogs, cats, rabbits and humans. Yellow-gray scales may be found on the back and the rump, top of the head and the nose.

## To Breed or Not To Breed

More than likely your breeder has requested that you have your puppy neutered or spayed. Your breeder's request is based on what is healthiest for your dog and what is most beneficial for your breed. Experienced and conscientious breeders devote many years into developing a bloodline. In order to do this, he makes every effort to plan each breeding in regard to conformation, temperament and health. This type of breeder does his best to perform the necessary testing (i.e., OFA, CERF, testing for inherited blood disorders, thyroid, etc.). Testing is expensive and sometimes very disheartening when a favorite dog doesn't pass his health tests. The health history pertains not only to the breeding stock but to the immediate ancestors. Reputable breeders do not want their offspring to be bred indiscriminately. Therefore you may be asked to neuter or spay your puppy. Of course there is always the exception, and your breeder may agree to let you breed your dog under his direct supervision. This is an important concept. More and more effort is being made to breed healthier dogs.

*The Basset's strong sense of smell may lead him far from home, so a fenced yard is important to his well being. These two potential wanderers are thinking about taking a hike!*

## Spay/Neuter

There are numerous benefits of performing this surgery at six months of age. Unspayed females are subject to mammary and ovarian cancer. In order to prevent mammary cancer she must be spayed prior to her first heat cycle. Later in life, an unspayed female may develop a pyometra (an infected uterus), which is definitely life threatening.

Spaying is performed under a general anesthetic and is easy on the young dog. As you might expect it is a little harder on the older dog, but that is no reason to deny her the surgery. The surgery removes the ovaries and uterus. It is important to remove all the ovarian tissue. If some is left behind, she could remain attractive to males. In order to view the ovaries, a reasonably long incision is necessary. An ovariohysterectomy is considered major surgery.

Neutering the male at a young age will inhibit some characteristic male behavior that owners frown upon. I have found my boys will not hike their legs and mark territory if they are neutered at six months of age. Also neutering at a young age has hormonal benefits, lessening the chance of hormonal aggressiveness.

Surgery involves removing the testicles but leaving the scrotum. If there should be a retained testicle, then he definitely needs to be neutered before the age of two or three years. Retained testicles can develop into cancer. Unneutered males are at risk for testicular cancer, perineal fistulas, perianal tumors and fistulas and prostatic disease.

Intact males and females are prone to housebreaking accidents. Females urinate frequently before, during and after heat cycles, and males tend to mark territory if there is a female in heat. Males may show the same behavior if there is a visiting dog or guests.

Surgery involves a sterile operating procedure equivalent to human surgery. The incision site is shaved, surgically scrubbed and draped. The veterinarian wears a sterile surgical gown, cap, mask and gloves. Anesthesia should be monitored by a registered technician. It is customary for the veterinarian to recommend a pre-anesthetic blood screening, looking for metabolic problems and a ECG rhythm strip to check for normal heart function. Today anesthetics are equal to human anesthetics, which enables your dog to walk out of the clinic the same day as surgery.

Some folks worry about their dog gaining weight after being neutered or spayed. This is usually not the case. It is true that some dogs may be less active so they could develop a problem, but my own dogs are just as active as they were before surgery. I have a hard time keeping weight on them. However, if your dog should begin to gain, then you need to decrease his food and see to it that he gets a little more exercise.

# DENTAL CARE for Your Dog's Life

So, you have a new puppy! Anyone who has ever raised a puppy is abundantly aware of how this new arrival affects the household. Your puppy will chew anything he can reach, chase your shoelaces, and play "tear the rag" with any piece of clothing he can find. When puppies are newly born, they have no teeth. At about four weeks of age, puppies of most breeds begin to develop their deciduous or baby teeth. They begin eating semi-solid food, biting and fighting with their littermates, and learning discipline from their mother. As their new teeth come in, they inflict pain on their mother's breasts, so feeding sessions become less frequent and shorter. By six or eight weeks, the mother will start growling to warn her pups when they are fighting too roughly or hurting her as they nurse too much with their new teeth.

*Casey "ate" the bat! Teething puppies will chew on anything, so be sure to puppy-proof your home and provide our Basset pup with plenty of safe toys.*

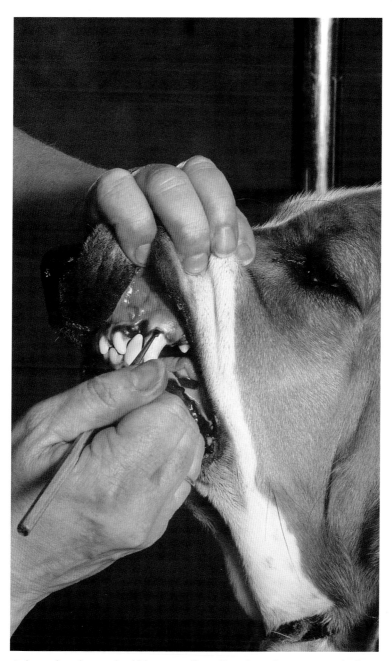

*A thorough oral exam should be a part of your Basset's regular veterinary check up.*

*If you keep your Basset Hound's teeth clean and free of plaque you will never have to worry about "doggy breath."*

*All dogs need safe chew toys to keep their teeth and jaws occupied.*

Puppies need to chew. It is a necessary part of their physical and mental development. They develop muscles and necessary life skills as they drag objects around, fight over possessions, and vocalize alerts and warnings. Puppies chew on things to explore their world. They are using their sense of taste to determine what is food and what is not. How else can they tell an electrical cord from a lizard? At about four months of age, most puppies begin shedding their baby teeth. Often, these teeth need some help to come out to make way for the permanent teeth. The incisors (front teeth) will be replaced first. Then, the adult canine or fang teeth erupt. When a baby tooth is not shed before the permanent tooth comes in, veterinarians call it a retained deciduous tooth. This condition will often cause gum infections by trapping hair and debris between the permanent tooth and the retained baby tooth. Puppies that are given adequate chew toys will exhibit less destructive behavior, develop more physically, and have less chance of retained deciduous teeth.

During the first year, your dog should be seen by your veterinarian at regular intervals. He will let you know when to bring your puppy in for vaccinations and parasite examinations. At each visit, your vet should inspect the lips, teeth, and mouth as part of a complete physical examination. You should take some part in the maintenance of your dog's oral health. Examine your dog's mouth weekly throughout his first year to make sure there are no sores, foreign objects, tooth problems, etc. If your dog drools excessively, shakes his head, or has bad breath, consult your veterinarian. By the time your dog is six months old, his permanent teeth are all in and plaque can start to accumulate on the tooth surfaces. This is when your dog needs good dental-care habits to prevent calculus buildup on his teeth. Brushing is best—that is a fact that cannot be denied. However, some dogs do not like their teeth brushed regularly, or you may not be able to accomplish the task. In this case, you should consider a product that will help prevent plaque and calculus

*Your Basset Hound will thrive with good health care, nutrition, and grooming.*

buildup, like any of the dental devices available from Nylabone®.

By the time dogs are four years old, 75 percent of them have periodontal disease. It is the most common infection in dogs. Yearly examinations by your vet are essential to maintaining your dog's

*Toys, like Nylabones®, will help keep your Basset Hound's teeth clean while keeping him busy and out of mischief.*

good health. If he detects periodontal disease, he or she may recommend a prophylactic cleaning. To do a thorough cleaning, it will be necessary to put your dog under anesthesia. With modern gas anesthetics and monitoring equipment, the procedure is pretty safe. Your veterinarian will scale the teeth with an ultrasound scaler or hand instrument. This removes the calculus from the teeth. If there are calculus deposits below the gum line, the veterinarian will plane the roots to make them smooth. After all of the calculus has been removed, the teeth are polished with pumice in a polishing cup. If any medical or surgical treatment is needed, it is done at this time. The final step would be fluoride treatment and your follow-up treatment

*Check your Basset Hound's teeth and mouth as part of his regular grooming routine.*

at home. If the periodontal disease is advanced, the veterinarian may prescribe a medicated mouth rinse or antibiotics for use at home. Make sure your dog has safe, clean, and attractive chew toys, like Nylabones®, and healthy treats.

As your dog ages, professional examination and cleaning should become more frequent. The mouth should be inspected at least once a year. Your vet may recommend visits every six months. In the geriatric patient, organs such as the heart, liver, and kidneys do not function as well as when your dog was young. Your vet will probably want to test these organs' functions

*Treats and toys can be used as rewards in training sessions.*

*A Basset Hound's teeth should be very large, white and strong. Terri Hennessy's "Bubba" flashes his pearly whites for the camera.*

prior to using general anesthesia for dental cleaning. If your dog is a good chewer and you work closely with your vet, he can keep all of his teeth all of his life. However, as your dog ages, his sense of smell, sight, and taste will diminish. He may not have the desire to chase, trap, or chew his toys. He will also not have the energy to chew for long periods, as arthritis and periodontal disease could make chewing painful. This will leave you with more responsibility for keeping his teeth clean and healthy. The dog that would not let you brush his teeth at one year of age, may let you brush his teeth now that he is ten years old.

If you train your dog with good chewing habits as a puppy, he will have healthier teeth throughout his life.

# IDENTIFICATION and Finding the Lost Dog

by Judy Iby

There are several ways of identifying your dog. The old standby is a collar with dog license, rabies, and ID tags. Unfortunately collars have a way of being separated from the dog and tags fall off. I am not suggesting you shouldn't use a collar and tags. If they stay intact and on the dog, they are the quickest way of identification.

For several years owners have been tattooing their dogs. Some tattoos use a number with a registry. Here lies the problem because there are several registries to check. If you wish to tattoo, use your social security number. The humane shelters have the means to trace it. It is usually done on the inside of the rear thigh. The area is first shaved and numbed. There is no pain, although a few dogs do not like the buzzing sound. Occasionally tattooing is not legible and needs to be redone.

The newest method of identification is microchipping. The microchip is a computer chip that is no larger than a grain of rice. The veterinarian implants it by injection between the shoulder blades. The dog feels no discomfort. If your dog is lost and picked up by the humane society, they can trace you by scanning the microchip, which has its own code. Microchip scanners are friendly

*Make sure you leave your Basset Hound in a secure fenced-in area when he is outdoors and off-lead.*

*Neither rain, sleet nor snow will deter the persistent Basset from his goal. This persistent fellow is owned by Marina Zacharias.*

to other brands of microchips and their registries. The microchip comes with a dog tag saying the dog is microchipped. It is the safest way of identifying your dog.

## FINDING THE LOST DOG

I am sure you will agree with me that there would be little worse than losing your dog. Responsible pet owners rarely lose their dogs. They do not let their dogs run free because they don't want harm to come to them. Not only that but in most, if not all, states there is a leash law.

Beware of fenced-in yards. They can be a hazard. Dogs find ways to escape either over or under the fence. Another fast exit is through the gate that perhaps the neighbor's child left unlocked.

Below is a list that hopefully will be of help to you if you need it. Remember don't give up, keep looking. Your dog is worth your efforts.

1. Contact your neighbors and put flyers with a photo on it in their mailboxes. Information you should include would be the dog's name, breed, sex, color, age, source of identification,

*Basset Hounds are famous for following their noses—which can lead to wandering off. A fenced-in yard is a must.*

*Always keep your dog on lead when outside to prevent him from becoming separated from you.*

when your dog was last seen and where, and your name and phone numbers. It may be helpful to say the dog needs medical care. Offer a *reward*.

2. Check all local shelters daily. It is also possible for your dog to be picked up away from home and end up in an out-of-the-way shelter. Check these too. Go in person. It is not good enough to call. Most shelters are limited on the time they can hold dogs then they are put up for adoption or euthanized. There is the possibility that your dog will not make it to the shelter for several days. Your dog could have been wandering or someone may have tried to keep him.

3. Notify all local veterinarians. Call and send flyers.

4. Call your breeder. Frequently breeders are contacted when one of their breed is found.

5. Contact the rescue group for your breed.

6. Contact local schools—children may have seen your dog.

7. Post flyers at the schools, groceries, gas stations, convenience stores, veterinary clinics, groomers and any other place that will allow them.

8. Advertise in the newspaper.

9. Advertise on the radio.

# TRAVELING with Your Basset Hound

### by Judy Iby

The earlier you start traveling with your new puppy or dog, the better. He needs to become accustomed to traveling. However, some dogs are nervous riders and become carsick easily. It is helpful if he starts with an empty stomach. Do not despair, as it will go better if you continue taking him with you on short fun rides. How would you feel if every time you rode in the car you stopped at the doctor's for an injection? You would soon dread that nasty car. Older dogs that tend to get carsick may have more of a problem adjusting to traveling. Those dogs that are having a serious problem may benefit from some medication prescribed by the veterinarian.

Do give your dog a chance to relieve himself before getting into the car. It is a good idea to be prepared for a clean up with a leash, paper towels, bag and terry cloth towel.

The safest place for your dog is in a fiberglass crate, although close confinement can promote carsickness in some dogs. If your dog is nervous you can try letting him ride on the seat next to you or in someone's lap.

*Begin traveling with your Basset Hound early in his life to accustom him to rides in the car. These three wait patiently for their ride.*

*The versatile Basset is pretty much a "go anywhere" kind of dog. This seasoned sailor is owned by Jackie Conway.*

An alternative to the crate would be to use a car harness made for dogs and/or a safety strap attached to the harness or collar. Whatever you do, do not let your dog ride in the back of a pickup truck unless he is securely tied on a very short lead. I've seen trucks stop quickly and, even though the dog was tied, it fell out and was dragged.

I do occasionally let my dogs ride loose with me because I really enjoy their companionship, but in all honesty they are safer in their crates. I have a friend whose van rolled in an accident but his dogs, in their fiberglass crates, were not injured nor did they escape. Another advantage of the crate is that it is a safe place to leave him if you need to run into the store. Otherwise you wouldn't be able to leave the windows down. Keep in mind that while many dogs are overly protective in their crates, this may not be enough to deter dognappers. In some states it is against the law to leave a dog in the car unattended.

*If you accustom your Basset Hound to car rides slowly, he will soon grow to enjoy them. "Guy" is learning to be a good passenger.*

Never leave a dog loose in the car wearing a collar and leash. I have known more than one dog that has killed himself by hanging. Do not let him put his head out an open window. Foreign debris can be blown into his eyes. When leaving your dog unattended in a car, consider the temperature. It can take less than five minutes to reach temperatures over 100 degrees Fahrenheit.

## TRIPS

Perhaps you are taking a trip. Give consideration to what is best for your dog—traveling with you or boarding. When traveling by car, van or motor home, you need to think ahead about locking your vehicle. In all probability you have many valuables in the car and do not wish to leave it unlocked. Perhaps most valuable and not replaceable is your dog. Give thought to securing your vehicle and providing adequate ventilation for him. Another consideration for you when traveling with your dog is medical problems that may arise and little inconveniences, such as exposure to external parasites. Some areas of the country are quite flea infested. You may want to carry flea spray with you. This is even a good idea when staying in motels. Quite possibly you are not the only occupant of the room.

Unbelievably many motels and even hotels do allow canine guests, even some very first-class ones. Gaines Pet Foods Corporation publishes *Touring With Towser*, a directory of domestic hotels and motels that

*You may consider boarding your dog at a reputable kennel if you plan to go on vacation.*

accommodate guests with dogs. Their address is Gaines TWT, PO Box 5700, Kankakee, IL, 60902. I would recommend you call ahead to any motel that you may be considering and see if they accept pets. Sometimes it is necessary to pay a deposit against room damage. Of course you are more likely to gain accommodations for a small dog than a large dog. Also the management feels reassured when you mention that your dog will be crated. Since my dogs tend to bark when I leave the room, I leave the TV on nearly full blast to deaden the noises outside that tend to encourage my dogs to bark. If you do travel with your dog, take along plenty of baggies so that you can clean up after him. When we all do our share in cleaning up, we make it possible for motels to continue accepting our pets. As a matter of fact, you should practice cleaning up everywhere you take your dog.

Depending on where your are traveling, you may need an up-to-date health certificate issued by your veterinarian. It is good policy to take along your dog's medical information, which would include the name, address and phone number of your veterinarian, vaccination record, rabies certificate, and any medication he is taking.

*The Basset Hound is very accepting and adapts well to any situation. This Basset's mellow character is in full bloom!*

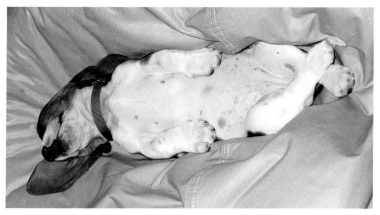

*Bassets are such accommodating dogs, they can get comfortable practically anywhere!*

## AIR TRAVEL

When traveling by air, you need to contact the airlines to check their policy. Usually you have to make arrangements up to a couple of weeks in advance for traveling with your dog. The airlines require your dog to travel in an airline approved fiberglass crate. Usually these can be purchased through the airlines but they are also readily available in most pet-supply stores. If your dog is not accustomed to a crate, then it is a good idea to get him acclimated to it before your trip. The day of the actual trip you should withhold water about one hour ahead of departure and no food for about 12 hours. The airlines generally have temperature restrictions, which do not allow pets to travel if it is either too cold or too hot. Frequently these restrictions are based on the temperatures at the departure and arrival airports. It's best to inquire about a health certificate. These usually need to be issued within ten days of departure. You should arrange for non-stop, direct flights and if a commuter plane should be involved, check to see if it will carry dogs. Some don't. The Humane Society of the United States has put together a tip sheet for airline traveling. You can receive a copy by sending a self-addressed stamped envelope to:

The Humane Society of the United States
Tip Sheet
2100 L Street NW
Washington, DC 20037.

Regulations differ for traveling outside of the country and are sometimes changed without notice. Well in advance you need to

*Most airlines and hotels have policies concerning traveling with pets, so be sure to check it out thoroughly before making any plans.*

write or call the appropriate consulate or agricultural department for instructions. Some countries have lengthy quarantines (six months), and countries differ in their rabies vaccination requirements. For instance, it may have to be given at least 30 days ahead of your departure.

Do make sure your dog is wearing proper identification. You never know when you might be in an accident and separated from your dog. Or your dog could be frightened and somehow manage to escape and run away. When I travel, my dogs wear collars with engraved nameplates with my name, phone number and city.

Another suggestion would be to carry in-case-of-emergency instructions. These would include the address and phone number of a relative or friend, your veterinarian's name, address and phone number, and your dog's medical information.

## BOARDING KENNELS

Perhaps you have decided that you need to board your dog. Your veterinarian can recommend a good boarding facility or possibly a pet sitter that will come to your house. It is customary for the boarding kennel to ask for proof of vaccination for the DHLPP, rabies and bordetella vaccine. The bordetella should have been given within six months of boarding. This is for your protection. If they do not ask for this proof I would not board at their kennel. Ask about flea control. Those dogs that suffer flea-bite allergy can get in trouble at a boarding kennel. Unfortunately boarding kennels are limited on how much they are able to do.

For more information on pet sitting, contact NAPPS:
National Association of Professional Pet Sitters
1200 G Street, NW
Suite 760
Washington, DC 20005.

Our clinic has technicians that pet sit and technicians that board clinic patients in their homes. This may be an alternative for you. Ask your veterinarian if they have an employee that can help you. There is a definite advantage of having a technician care for your dog, especially if your dog is on medication or is a senior citizen.

You can write for a copy of *Traveling With Your Pet* from ASPCA, Education Department, 441 E. 92nd Street, New York, NY 10128.

# BEHAVIOR and Canine Communication

### by Judy Iby

S tudies of the human/animal bond point out the importance of the unique relationships that exist between people and their pets. Those of us who share our lives with pets understand the special part they play through companionship, service and protection. For many, the pet/owner bond goes beyond simple companionship; pets are often considered members of the family. A leading pet food manufacturer recently conducted a nationwide survey of pet owners to gauge just how important pets were in their lives. Here's what they found:

• 76 percent allow their pets to sleep on their beds
• 78 percent think of their pets as their children
• 84 percent display photos of their pets react to their own emotions
• 100 percent talk to their pets
• 97 percent think that their pets understand what they're saying
Are you surprised?

Senior citizens show more concern for their own eating habits when they have the responsibility of feeding a dog. Seeing that their dog is routinely exercised encourages the owner to think of schedules

*Interestingly, many Basset owners find two dogs easier than one. Rosemarie Peterson's nattily dressed pair are ready for a night on the town.*

*It has been found that spending quality time with a dog can reduce stress and improve your quality of life. Who could resist these adorable Bassets?*

*The ultimate house dog and companion, the Basset Hound enriches the lives of his owners.*

that otherwise may seem unimportant to the senior citizen. The older owner may be arthritic and feeling poorly but with responsibility for his dog he has a reason to get up and get moving. It is a big plus if his dog is an attention seeker who will demand such from his owner.

Over the last couple of decades, it has been shown that pets relieve the stress of those who lead busy lives. Owning a pet has been known to lessen the occurrence of heart attack and stroke.

Many single folks thrive on the companionship of a dog. Lifestyles are very different from a long time ago, and today more individuals seek the single life. However, they receive fulfillment from owning a dog.

Most likely the majority of our dogs live in family environments. The companionship they provide is well worth the effort involved.

In my opinion, every child should have the opportunity to have a family dog. Dogs teach responsibility through understanding their care, feelings and even respecting their life cycles. Frequently those children who have not been exposed to dogs grow up afraid of dogs, which isn't good. Dogs sense timidity and some will take advantage of the situation.

Today more dogs are serving as service dogs. Since the origination of the Seeing Eye dogs years ago, we now have trained hearing dogs. Also dogs are trained to provide service for the handicapped and are able to perform many different tasks for their owners. Search and Rescue dogs, with their handlers, are sent throughout the world to assist in recovery of disaster victims. They are life savers.

Therapy dogs are very popular with nursing homes, and some hospitals even allow them to visit. The inhabitants truly look forward to their visits. I have taken a couple of my dogs visiting and left in tears when I saw the response of the patients. They wanted and were allowed to have my dogs in their beds to hold and love.

Nationally there is a Pet Awareness Week to educate students and others about the value and basic care of our pets. Many countries take an even greater interest in their pets than Americans do. In those countries the pets are allowed to accompany their owners into restaurants and shops, etc. In the U.S. this freedom is

*There is nothing more convincing than the sad-looking eyes of the Basset Hound. Ch. Musicland's Ain't She Sweet shows her persuasive power.*

only available to our service dogs. Even so we think very highly of the human/animal bond.

## CANINE BEHAVIOR

Canine behavior problems are the number-one reason for pet owners to dispose of their dogs, either through new homes, humane shelters or euthanasia. Unfortunately there are too many owners who are unwilling to devote the necessary time to properly train their dogs. On the other hand, there are those who not only are concerned about inherited health problems but are also aware of the dog's mental stability.

You may realize that a breed and his group relatives (i.e., sporting, hounds, etc.) show tendencies to behavioral characteristics. An experienced breeder can acquaint you with his breed's personality. Unfortunately many breeds are labeled with poor temperaments when actually the breed as a whole is not affected but only a small percentage of individuals within the breed.

If the breed in question is very popular, then of course there may be a higher number of unstable dogs. Do not label a breed good or bad. I know of absolutely awful-tempered dogs within one of our most popular, lovable breeds.

Inheritance and environment contribute to the dog's behavior. Some naïve people suggest inbreeding as the cause of bad temperaments. Inbreeding only results in poor behavior if the

*A loving and playful relationship with his dam and littermates is the first step to a well-socialized Basset Hound.*

*Bassets are definitely intelligent, but intellectual? Jane Wilner's Sherlock looks as if he possesses the wisdom of the ages.*

ancestors carry the trait. If there are excellent temperaments behind the dogs, then inbreeding will promote good temperaments in the offspring. Did you ever consider that inbreeding is what sets the characteristics of a breed? A purebred dog is the end result of inbreeding. This does not spare the mixed-breed dog from the same problems. Mixed-breed dogs frequently are the offspring of purebred dogs.

When planning a breeding, I like to observe the potential stud and his offspring in the show ring. If I see unruly behavior, I try to look into it further. I want to know if it is genetic or environmental, due to the lack of training and socialization. A good breeder will avoid breeding mentally unsound dogs.

Not too many decades ago most of our dogs led a different lifestyle than what is prevalent today. Usually mom stayed home so the dog had human companionship and someone to discipline it if needed. Not much was expected from the dog. Today's mom works and everyone's life is at a much faster pace.

The dog may have to adjust to being a "weekend" dog. The family is gone all day during the week, and the dog is left to his own devices for entertainment. Some dogs sleep all day waiting for their family to come home and others become wigwam wreckers if given the opportunity. Crates do ensure the safety of the dog and the house. However, he could become a physically and emotionally cripple if he doesn't get enough exercise and attention. We still appreciate and want the companionship of our dogs although we expect more from them. In many cases we tend to forget dogs are just that—*dogs* not human beings.

I own several dogs who are left crated during the day but I do try to make time for them in the evenings and on the weekends. Also we try to do something together before I leave for work. Maybe it helps them to have the companionship of other dogs. They accept their crates as their personal "houses" and seem to be content with their routine and thrive on trying their best to please me.

## Socializing and Training

Many prospective puppy buyers lack experience regarding the proper socialization and training needed to develop the type of pet we all desire. In the first 18 months, training does take some work. Trust me, it is easier to start proper training before there is a problem that needs to be corrected.

The initial work begins with the breeder. The breeder should start socializing the puppy at five to six weeks of age and cannot let up. Human socializing is critical up through 12 weeks of age and likewise important during the following months. The litter should

*The more people and animals your dog meets—including other Bassets—the better socialized he will become.*

*If you introduce your Basset to other pets carefully, they will soon get along famously. Minibus and her feline friend Queenie are regular bed partners.*

be left together during the first few weeks but it is necessary to separate them by ten weeks of age. Leaving them together after that time will increase competition for litter dominance. If puppies are not socialized with people by 12 weeks of age, they will be timid in later life.

The eight- to ten-week age period is a fearful time for puppies. They need to be handled very gently around children and adults. There should be no harsh discipline during this time. Starting at 14 weeks of age, the puppy begins the juvenile period, which ends when he reaches sexual maturity around six to 14 months of age. During the juvenile period he needs to be introduced to strangers (adults, children and other dogs) on the home property. At sexual maturity he will begin to bark at strangers and become more protective. Males start to lift their legs to urinate but if you desire you can inhibit this behavior by walking your boy on leash away from trees, shrubs, fences, etc.

Perhaps you are thinking about an older puppy. You need to inquire about the puppy's social experience. If he has lived in a kennel, he may have a hard time adjusting to people and environmental stimuli. Assuming he has had a good social upbringing, there are advantages to an older puppy.

*While this handsome Basset has every confidence in the world that the skipper can run the ship, it's better to be safe than sorry.*

Training includes puppy kindergarten and a minimum of one to two basic training classes. During these classes you will learn how to dominate your youngster. This is especially important if you own a large breed of dog. It is somewhat harder, if not nearly impos-

*There are few breeds as easy going as the Basset Hound. This Christmas trio is owned by Lynn Miller.*

sible, for some owners to be the Alpha figure when their dog towers over them. You will be taught how to properly restrain your dog. This concept is important. Again it puts you in the Alpha position. All dogs need to be restrained many times during their lives. Believe it or not, some of our worst offenders are the eight-week-old puppies that are brought to our clinic. They need to be gently restrained for a nail trim but the way they carry on you would think we were killing them. In comparison, their vaccination is a "piece of cake." When we ask dogs to do something that is not agreeable to them, then their worst comes out. Life will be easier for your dog if you expose him at a young age to the necessities of life—proper behavior and restraint.

*Keep your Basset Hound occupied by giving him Nylafloss®. It does wonders for your dog's dental health by massaging his gums and literally flossing between his teeth.*

## UNDERSTANDING THE DOG'S LANGUAGE

Most authorities agree that the dog is a descendent of the wolf. The dog and wolf have similar traits. For instance both are pack oriented and prefer not to be isolated for long periods of time. Another characteristic is that the dog, like the wolf, looks to the leader—Alpha—for direction. Both the wolf and the dog communicate through body language, not only within their pack but with outsiders.

Every pack has an Alpha figure. The dog looks to you, or should look to you, to be that leader. If your dog doesn't receive the proper training and guidance, he very well may replace you as Alpha. This would be a serious problem and is certainly a disservice to your dog.

Eye contact is one way the Alpha wolf keeps order within his pack. You are Alpha so you must establish eye contact with your puppy. Obviously your puppy will have to look at you. Practice eye contact even if you need to hold his head for five to ten seconds at a time. You can give him a treat as a reward. Make sure your eye contact is gentle and not threatening. Later, if he has been naughty, it is permissible to give him a long, penetrating look. I caution you there are some older dogs that never learned eye contact as puppies and cannot accept eye contact. You should avoid eye contact with these dogs since they feel threatened and will retaliate as such.

*A basketful of Bassets owned by Grace Servais of Switzerland.*

*Your Basset may try to declare his independence, but he should always know that you're the boss.*

## BODY LANGUAGE

The play bow, when the forequarters are down and the hindquarters are elevated, is an invitation to play. Puppies play fight, which helps them learn the acceptable limits of biting. This is necessary for later in their lives. Nevertheless, an owner may be falsely reassured by the playful nature of his dog's aggression. Playful aggression toward another dog or human may be an indication of serious aggression in the future. Owners should never play fight or play tug-of-war with any dog that is inclined to be dominant.

Signs of submission are:

1. Avoids eye contact.

2. Active submission—the dog crouches down, ears back and the tail is lowered.

3. Passive submission—the dog rolls on his side with his hindlegs in the air and frequently urinates.

Signs of dominance are:

1. Makes eye contact.

2. Stands with ears up, tail up and the hair raised on his neck.

3. Shows dominance over another dog by standing at right angles over it.

Dominant dogs tend to behave in characteristic ways such as:

1. The dog may be unwilling to move from his place (i.e., reluctant to give up the sofa if the owner wants to sit there).

2. He may not part with toys or objects in his mouth and may show possessiveness with his food bowl.

3. He may not respond quickly to commands.

4. He may be disagreeable for grooming and dislikes to be petted.

Dogs are popular because of their sociable nature. Those that have contact with humans during the first 12 weeks of life regard them as a member of their own species—their pack. All dogs have the potential for both dominant and submissive behavior. Only through experience and training do they learn to whom it is appropriate to show which behavior. Not all dogs are concerned with dominance but owners need to be aware of that potential. It is wise for the owner to establish his dominance early on.

A human can express dominance or submission toward a dog in the following ways:

1. Meeting the dog's gaze signals dominance. Averting the gaze signals submission. If the dog growls or threatens, averting the

*Although he may seem like the perfect gift, the holidays are the worst time to bring a new puppy into your household. Rudy is owned by Lynn and Sara Hollabaugh.*

*Well-cared-for Basset Hounds can live to a ripe old age and become more endearing as the years pass. This elderly gentleman is owned by Dave and Geneva Koch.*

gaze is the first avoiding action to take—it may prevent attack. It is important to establish eye contact in the puppy. The older dog that has not been exposed to eye contact may see it as a threat and will not be willing to submit.

2. Being taller than the dog signals dominance; being lower signals submission. This is why, when attempting to make friends with a strange dog or catch the runaway, one should kneel down to his level. Some owners see their dogs become dominant when allowed on the furniture or on the bed. Then he is at the owner's level.

3. An owner can gain dominance by ignoring all the dog's social initiatives. The owner pays attention to the dog only when he obeys a command.

No dog should be allowed to achieve dominant status over any adult or child. Ways of preventing are as follows:

1. Handle the puppy gently, especially during the three- to four-month period.

2. Let the children and adults handfeed him and teach him to take food without lunging or grabbing.

3. Do not allow him to chase children or joggers.

4. Do not allow him to jump on people or mount their legs. Even females may be inclined to mount. It is not only a male habit.

5. Do not allow him to growl for any reason.

6. Don't participate in wrestling or tug-of-war games.

7. Don't physically punish puppies for aggressive behavior. Restrain him from repeating the infraction and teach an alternative behavior. Dogs should earn everything they receive from their owners. This would include sitting to receive petting or treats, sitting before going out the door and sitting to receive the collar and leash. These types of exercises reinforce the owner's dominance.

Young children should never be left alone with a dog. It is important that children learn some basic obedience commands so they have some control over the dog. They will gain the respect of their dog.

## Fear

One of the most common problems dogs experience is being fearful. Some dogs are more afraid than others. On the lesser side, which is sometimes humorous to watch, my dog can be afraid of a strange object. He acts silly when some-thing is out of place in the house. I call his problem perceptive intelligence. He realizes the abnormal within his known environment. He does not react the same way in strange environments since he does not know what is normal.

On the more serious side is a fear of people. This can result in backing off, seeking his own space and saying "leave me alone" or it can result in an aggressive behavior that may lead to challenging the person. Respect that the dog wants to be left alone and give him time to come forward. If you approach the cornered dog, he may resort to snapping. If you leave him alone, he may decide to come forward, which should be rewarded with a treat. Years ago we had a dog that behaved in this manner. We coaxed people to stop by the house and make friends with our fearful dog. She learned to take the treats and after weeks of

*A clown and a court jester, even without the costume! John and Jackie Conway have a comedian on their hands every day of their lives.*

work she overcame her suspicions and made friends more readily.

Some dogs may initially be too fearful to take treats. In these cases it is helpful to make sure the dog hasn't eaten for about 24 hours. Being a little hungry encourages him to accept the treats, especially if they are of the "gourmet" variety. I have a dog that worries about strangers since people seldom stop by my house. Over the years she has learned a cue and jumps up quickly to visit anyone sitting on the sofa. She learned by herself that all guests on the sofa were to be trusted friends. I think she felt more comfortable with them being at her level, rather than towering over her.

Dogs can be afraid of numerous things, including loud noises and thunderstorms. Invariably the owner rewards (by comforting) the dog when it shows signs of fearfulness. I had a terrible problem with my favorite dog in the Utility obedience class. Not only was he intimidated in the class but he was afraid of noise and afraid of displeasing me. Frequently he would knock down the bar jump, which clattered dreadfully. I gave him credit because he continued to try to clear it, although he was terribly scared. I finally learned to "reward" him every time he knocked down the jump. I would jump up and down, clap my hands and tell him how great he was. My psychology worked, he relaxed and eventually cleared the jump with ease. When your dog is frightened, direct his attention to something else and act happy. Don't dwell on his fright.

## AGGRESSION

Some different types of aggression are: predatory, defensive, dominance, possessive, protective, fear induced, noise provoked, "rage" syndrome (unprovoked aggression), maternal and aggression directed toward other dogs. Aggression is the most common behavioral problem encountered. Protective breeds are expected to be more aggressive than others but with the proper upbringing they can make very dependable companions. You need to be able to read your dog.

Many factors contribute to aggression including genetics and environment. An im-proper environment, which may include the living conditions, lack of social life, excessive punishment, being attacked or frightened by an aggressive dog, etc., can all influence a dog's behavior. Even spoiling him and giving too much praise may be detrimental. Isolation and the lack of human contact or exposure to frequent teasing by children or adults also can ruin a good dog.

Lack of direction, fear, or confusion lead to aggression in those dogs that are so inclined. Any obedience exercise, even the sit and down, can direct the dog and overcome fear and/or confusion. Every dog should learn these commands as a youngster, and there should be periodic reinforcement.

When a dog is showing signs of aggression, you should speak calmly (no screaming or hysterics) and firmly give a command that he understands, such as the sit. As soon as your dog obeys, you have assumed your dominant position. Aggression presents a problem because there may be danger to others. Sometimes it is an emotional issue. Owners may consciously or unconsciously encourage their dog's aggression. Other owners show responsibility by accepting the problem and taking measures to keep it under control. The owner is responsible for his dog's actions, and it is not wise to take a chance on someone being bitten, especially a child. Euthanasia is the solution for some owners and in severe cases this may be the best choice. However, few dogs are that dangerous and very few are that much of a threat to their owners. If caution is exercised and

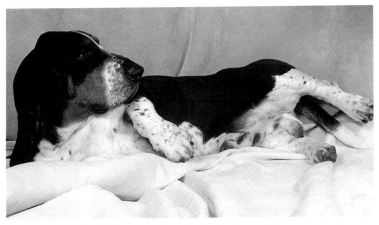

*This Basset Hound's body language shows he is submissive to his owner, and he wants a tummy rub!*

professional help is gained early on, then I surmise most cases can be controlled.

Some authorities recommend feeding a lower protein (less than 20 percent) diet. They believe this can aid in reducing aggression. If the dog loses weight, then vegetable oil can be added. Veterinarians and behaviorists are having some success with pharmacology. In many cases treatment is possible and can improve the situation.

If you have done everything according to "the book" regarding training and socializing and are still having a behavior problem, don't procrastinate. It is important that the problem gets attention before it is out of hand. It is estimated that 20 percent of a veterinarian's time may be devoted to dealing with problems before they become so intolerable that the dog is separated from its home and owner. If your veterinarian isn't able to help, he should refer you to a behaviorist.

## PROBLEMS

### Barking

This is a habit that shouldn't be encouraged. Over the years I've had new puppy owners call to say that their dog hasn't learned to bark. I assure them they are indeed fortunate but not to worry. Some owners desire their dog to bark so as to be a watchdog. In my experience, most dogs will bark when a stranger comes to the door.

The new puppy frequently barks or whines in the crate in his strange environment and the owner reinforces the puppy's bad behavior by going to him during the night. This is a no-no. I tell my new owners to smack the top of the crate and say "quiet" in a loud, firm voice. The puppies don't like to hear the loud noise of the crate being banged. If the barking is sleep-interrupting, then the owner should take crate and pup to the bedroom for a few days until the puppy becomes adjusted to his new environment. Otherwise ignore the barking during the night.

Barking can be an inherited problem or a bad habit learned through the environment. It takes dedication to stop the barking. Attention should be paid to the cause of the barking. Does the dog seek attention, does he need to go out, is it feeding time, is it occurring when he is left alone, is it a protective bark, etc.? Presently I have a ten-week-old puppy that is a real loud mouth, which I am sure is an inherited tendency. Both her mother and especially her grandmother are overzealous barkers but fortunately have mellowed with the years. My young puppy is corrected with a firm "no" and gentle shaking and she is responding. When barking presents a problem for you, try to stop it as soon as it begins.

There are electronic collars available that are supposed to curb barking. Personally I have not had experience with them. There are some disadvantages to to the collar. If the dog is barking out of excitement, punishment is not the appropriate treatment. Presumably there is the chance the collar could be activated by other stimuli and thereby punish the dog when it is not barking. Should you decide to use one, then you should seek help from a person with experience with that type of collar. In my opinion I feel the root of the problem needs to be investigated and corrected.

In extreme circumstances (usually when there is a problem with the neighbors), some people have resorted to having their dogs debarked. I caution you that the dog continues to bark but usually only a squeaking sound is heard. Frequently the vocal cords grow back. Probably the biggest concern is that the dog can be left with scar tissue which can narrow the opening to the trachea.

# RESOURCES

**Basset Hound Club of America**
1911 W. 11th St.
Anderson, IN 46016-2370
765-642-1495
www.basset-bhca.org

**American Kennel Club**
5580 Centerview Dr., Ste. 200
Raleigh, NC 27606
www.akc.org

**United Kennel Club**
100 E. Kilgore Rd.
Kalamazoo, MI 49002-5584
616-393-9020
www.UKC.org

**North American Dog Agility Council, Inc.**
HCR @ Box 277
St. Maries, ID 83861
972-231-9700

**US Dog Agility Association**
P.O. Box 850955
Richardson, TX 75085-0955
214-231-9700

**The American Rabbit Hunter Association**
P.O. Box 557
Royston, GA 30662
706-245-0081
http:www.arha.com

# INDEX